Physical Characteristics of the Tibetan Terrier

(from the American Kennel Club breed standard)

Body: Compact, square and strong, capable of both speed and endurance.

Topline: The back is level in motion.

Tail: Medium length, heavily furnished, set on fairly high and falls forward over the back, may curl to either side. There may be a kink near the tip.

Hindquarters: *Legs*—Well furnished, with well bent stifles and the hind legs are slightly longer than the forelegs. *Thighs*—Relatively broad and well muscled. *Hocks*—Low set and turn neither in nor out.

Coat: Double coat. Undercoat is soft and woolly. Outer coat is profuse and fine but never silky or woolly. May be wavy or straight. Coat is long but should not hang to the ground. A natural part is often present over the neck and back.

Color: Any color or combination of colors including white is acceptable to the breed.

Feet: Large, flat, and round in shape producing a snowshoe effect that provides traction. The pads are thick and strong. They are heavily furnished with hair between the toes and pads. The dog should stand well down on its pads.

Size: Average weight is 20 to 24 pounds, but the weight range may be 18 to 30 pounds. The average height in dogs is 15 to 16 inches, bitches slightly smaller.

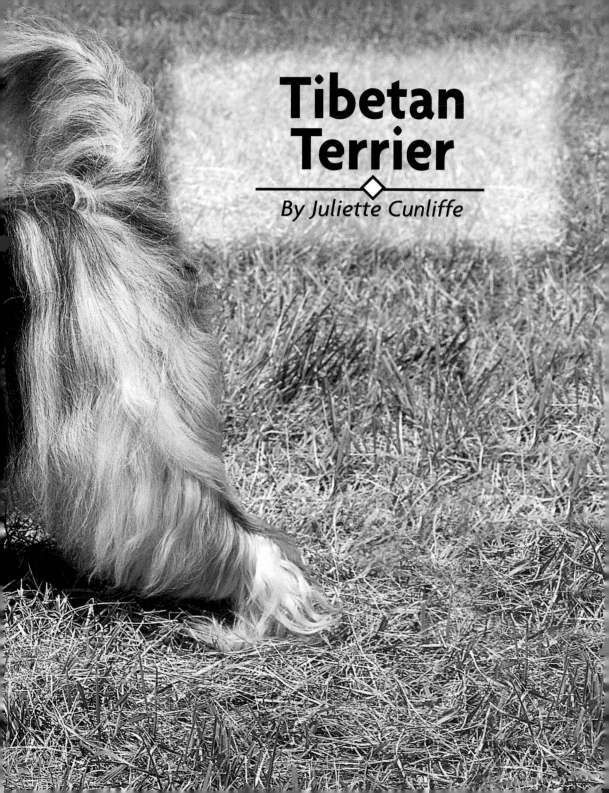

Tibetan Terrier

By Juliette Cunliffe

Contents

Training Your Tibetan Terrier   93

Begin with the basics of training the puppy and adult dog. Learn the principles of house-training the Tibetan Terrier, including the use of crates and basic scent instincts. Enter puppy kindergarten and introduce the pup to his collar and leash and progress to the basic commands. Find out about obedience classes and other activities.

Healthcare of Your Tibetan Terrier   117

By Lowell Ackerman DVM, DACVD
Become your dog's healthcare advocate and a well-educated canine keeper. Select a skilled and able veterinarian. Discuss pet insurance, vaccinations and infectious diseases, the neuter/spay decision and a sensible, effective plan for parasite control, including fleas, ticks and worms.

Showing Your Tibetan Terrier   142

Step into the center ring and find out about the world of showing pure-bred dogs. Here's how to get started in AKC shows, how they are organized and what's required for your dog to become a champion. Take a leap into the realms of obedience and agility tests.

KENNEL CLUB BOOKS® **TIBETAN TERRIER**
ISBN: 1-59378-275-6

Copyright © 2006 • Kennel Club Books, LLC
308 Main Street, Allenhurst, NJ 07711 USA
Cover Design Patented: US 6,435,559 B2 • Printed in South Korea

10 9 8 7 6 5 4 3 2 1

Photography by Carol Ann Johnson
with additional photographs by:

John Ashbey, Mary Bloom, K. Booth, Paulette Braun, Berndt Brinkmann, Carolina Biological Supply, Cook Studio, Juliette Cunliffe, Tara Darling, Isabelle Français, Leash to Lens Photo by Gilbert, Bill Jonas, Dr. Dennis Kunkel, Tam C. Nguyen, Phototake and Jean Claude Revy.

Illustrations by Patricia Peters.

The publisher wishes to thank all of the owners whose dogs are illustrated in this book, including Jackie Carrington, Juliette Cunliffe, Carol Ann Johnson, Cheryl and Dave Johnston, Anne Keleman, Dr. Mike Tempest and Tyras.

The Tibetan Terrier comes from Tibet, in the Himalayan Mountains, the highest range in the world. The breed has captured the hearts of many canine enthusiasts and is now found throughout the world.

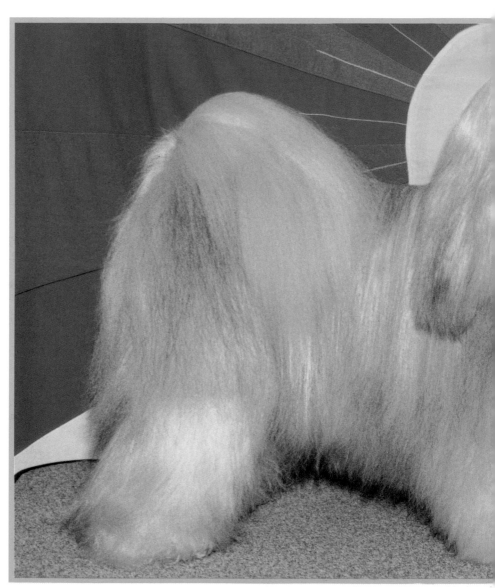

HISTORY OF THE

TIBETAN TERRIER

The Tibetan Terrier is an enchanting, hardy, intelligent and active breed that hails from "the Roof of the World," a mystical country with a barren landscape. The country's dogs, like its people, have to be able to deal with extremes of temperature, fiercely bright light and high altitude; the majority of Tibetans live at altitudes of between 10,000 and 16,000 feet.

Over the years, there has been some confusion between the Tibetan Terrier and its close cousin, the Lhasa Apso. This has been due, in part, to the fact that Tibetans refer to all small and reasonably small long-coated dogs as "Apsos." Indeed, even to this day, the British Museum houses a carefully preserved Lhasa Apso that is still labeled "Tibetan Terrier."

In the past, the general confusion caused some dogs to be described as being as small as Maltese Terriers, others as large as Russian Poodles. Clearly the discrepancies arose because there was, indeed, more than one breed. To further complicate matters, in the early years Tibetan Terriers were registered as Lhasa Terriers. Something all

TIBETAN TERRIER DEVOTION
In difficult times of famine, Tibetans would sell or exchange all their treasures, but so devoted were they to their dogs that they would never part with them. Tibetans only part with their dogs as gifts or for great services that have been rendered.

the dogs had in common was their tails that curled over their backs, a highly Tibetan characteristic of several different breeds known today.

The author travels regularly to the Himalayas to study the dogs and peoples of the region

The Lhasa Apso, a close relative of the Tibetan Terrier. The Lhasa Apso is normally seen with the hair covering its face to protect the dog's eyes from the wind, snow and flying sand particles.

and finds that, even there, the dividing line between the two breeds is often not clear. However, there is a clear distinction between typical specimens of each breed.

Around the turn of the 20th century, the smaller Lhasa Apso was slowly becoming known outside its homeland, but some enthusiasts were at pains to point out that in Tibet there was another larger breed of dog that was in many ways similar to it. This wonderful and worthy dog, of course, was the Tibetan Terrier.

Travelers had seen Tibetan Terriers gathering up flocks of sheep, rushing up the mountain at the signal from their owner and circling the sheep, rather as one might expect of a collie dog. The dogs were seen leaping from rock to rock, jumping with cat-like precision and seemingly without great effort.

There was no room for mistakes when a Tibetan Terrier was working in the mountainous Tibetan terrain, for the drops were precipitous and an error of judgment could all too easily spell death. This is the reason why the Tibetan Terrier is required to have large round feet which, as one can see from the breed standard, are quite differently constructed from those of most other dogs.

Because many of the anecdotal images about the

smaller Tibetan dogs might have referred to both the breed we now know as the Lhasa Apso as well as to the Tibetan Terrier, there has always been some element of debate about the actual functions of the respective breeds. There is no doubt, however, that Tibetan Terriers were certainly used to herd sheep and also to travel with pack animals. Frequently the drivers of pack animals over-indulged in spirits and became intoxicated, and it has been said that it was only the determination of their Tibetan Terriers that kept them on track. When a driver fell in the snow, his Tibetan Terrier would paw him to get up again

Perking the most unique ears in dogdom, the Hungarian Pumi is closely related to the Tibetan Terrier.

and move onward. These dogs were also reputed to be so agile that they were of great assistance in retrieving objects that had fallen into some inaccessible place along the treacherous path.

The Tibetan Terrier is closely allied to European and Asiatic herding dogs, including the Hungarian Puli and Pumi and the Polish Lowland Sheepdog. These three sheepdog breeds are all sized similarly to the Tibetan Terrier, and each has a unique full coat, though only the Puli's coat will cord. It is these cords that are the Hungarian Puli's hallmark, while the Pumi is known for its upright, forward-tipped ears and the Polish Lowland Sheepdog for its humanlike personality and intelligence. Like the Tibetan Terrier, all these breeds are excellent companions and

Historians cite the European sheepdogs as relations of the Tibetan Terrier. The Puli's hallmark is his corded coat.

The Polish Lowland Sheepdog, an irresistible breed that is fast gaining acceptance in Britain and around the world, is quite similar to the Tibetan Terrier in many respects.

watchdogs with affectionate, attentive personalities.

THE TIBETAN TERRIER TRAVELS TO THE UK

In 1922 Dr. Agnes R. H. Greig served in Cawnpore as a member of the Women's Medical Service of India. The rather amazing story of her introduction to the breed involves a Tibetan family arriving at the hospital with not only their goods and chattels but also their animals. The wife had a large

ATTENTION TO THE BREED

Miss Nye, living in India, owned the well-known Tibetan Terrier Puck. While on vacation in Kashmir, Puck saved her mistress from falling into the Jelhum River. Dr. Greig sent a report about this to England's *Daily Mirror* newspaper, thus drawing further attention to the breed.

ovarian cyst that required an operation, but the family was distraught that their dog, Lilly, was not allowed to stay in the hospital with her. As something of a compromise, Dr. Greig offered to keep Lilly in her own bungalow until the wife was well enough to look after her again. Undoubtedly, this Tibetan family had absolutely no idea of the impact they were about to make on the Tibetan Terrier world in the West.

When the woman had recovered, she invited Dr. Greig to have one of Lilly's puppies as a token of her gratitude. The one she selected was Bunti, a golden and white bitch. Dr. Greig already showed Pekingese, and when Bunti was a year old she approached the Indian Kennel Club to ask if she might show her, too. At first Bunti was not accepted by the Indian panel of judges as a Tibetan Terrier, but it was agreed that after three generations of careful breeding, the offspring should again be assessed.

Rajah was used as stud on Bunti, who produced her first litter of puppies on Christmas Day of 1924; indeed, he was also the sire of her second litter, whelped in 1925. The following year Dr. Greig went home to England for ten months' leave, taking Bunti, a bitch from the first litter and a dog from the second. These three dogs were registered with the English Kennel Club and recorded in the December 1926 issue of the *Kennel Gazette* (although Bunti's name was spelt Bunty).

In 1927 Bunti was mated to her son, Ja-Haz, and one of the three puppies, Mr. Binks, was taken back to India when Dr. Greig returned. Mr. Binks was to

Lieutenant Colonel Eric Bailey owned this Tibetan Terrier around 1930.

become the first Tibetan Terrier champion, having won four Challenge Certificates in India. It was finally agreed with the Indian Kennel Club that Dr. Greig's dogs were to be registered as a distinct breed, Tibetan Terriers.

In 1930 the Indian Kennel Club described a standard of points for the Tibetan Terrier, and the following year Tibetan Terriers were registered as such in the English Kennel Club's *Kennel Gazette*.

Miss Nye, a colleague and friend of Dr. Greig in Karachi, also became interested in Tibetan Terriers, and together the two ladies obtained a litter brother and sister. The bitch was owned by Dr. Greig, and the dog by Miss Nye. However, although Dr. Greig

HEATED MEETINGS

When the division of the Tibetan breeds was underway in the early 1930s, rather heated meetings were held at Lady Freda Valentine's London home. In her inimitable way, Lady Freda used to ask the formidable Dr. Agnes Greig if she would pass around the cream cakes. This caused her to be obliged to speak to others attending the meeting, and they to her, so breaking the ice.

had set her heart firmly upon developing the Tibetan Terrier, she had served in India for around 12 years and was feeling decidedly homesick. So it was that in the early 1930s she and Miss Nye set up a kennel on the Isle of Jersey after Dr. Greig had taken leave from the Women's Medical Service. Both ladies brought a few of their dogs back to Europe.

Around the same time, the Lhasa Apso fraternity was trying hard to keep their breed distinct from another of its close cousins, the Shih Tzu. Finally, the differences between those two breeds were resolved and the time was ripe to set up the Tibetan Breeds Association. In 1934 breed standards were laid down for the Lhasa Apso, Tibetan Terrier, Tibetan Spaniel and Tibetan

In 1932 the Tibetan Terrier was a true rarity in dog circles. The original caption that accompanied this photograph read: "It is rare to meet with Tibetan Terriers outside of Tibet, but Mrs. Greig's fine example of the breed, Ghoto Sahib of Ladkok, made its appearance at The Kennel Club Show in 1932."

GLAMOR IN THE SHOW RING

Dr. Greig, who did not agree with having Tibetan Terriers being glamorously presented for the show ring, was heard to remark, "they don't need a hairdresser to show them." A forthright lady who owned many Tibetans, Dr. Greig did not clip any of the coats for ease of management. This unfortunately resulted in a large number of heavily matted coats!

Mastiff. The Shih Tzu was classified as a separate breed and was not represented by the newly formed association.

Several new breeders became involved with the Tibetan Terrier, although the word "terrier" caused its own problems among many of the judges not familiar with the breed. The Tibetan Terrier has never been a terrier in the true sense of the word, a dog bred to go to ground after vermin, though in some countries the breed still finds itself classified in the Terrier Group. In the US as in the UK, the breed is classified as a Non-Sporting (Utility) breed, while in the Fédération Cynologique Internationale, the Tibetan Terrier is aptly classified as a Companion Dog.

The 1930s were sufficiently successful for the breed in Britain for The Kennel Club to announce, in October 1937, that it was going

to award Challenge Certificates for the breed at Crufts in 1938. This meant that the Tibetan Terrier had achieved championship status.

The Crufts catalog has long been renowned for its short descriptions of each breed classified at the show, and from this many people learn for the first time about a breed. The description likened Tibetan Terriers to small Bobtail sheepdogs and gave a weight range of between 16 and 30 lbs. The judge officiating for this breed at the show was Mrs. D. F. Gardiner, and in her critique she commented about the size discrepancy being somewhat disconcerting. Nevertheless, she remarked that the type was "well marked" and clearly she found the Tibetan Terrier a thoroughly attractive breed.

In the mid-1930s Dr. Greig moved to mainland England to join her mother in Royden, Essex. Her mother was already an established dog breeder, and the ladies' kennel names of Lamleh and Ladkok became increasingly well known throughout the world. Dr. Greig and her mother sent several Tibetan Terriers abroad during the latter part of the 1930s.

Mrs. Greig and her daughter Dr. Greig were among the most important Tibetan Terrier owners in Britain in the early period. They are photographed here with some of the dogs that Mrs. Greig bred and owned.

WORLD WAR II

Food was scarce during the war years, and, at the beginning of the war, dog shows were suspended. Just when the Tibetan Terrier had begun to achieve public acclaim, the war wrought havoc with people's breeding plans. Not all dog owners retained their stock during the war, but despite further losses caused by a distemper outbreak, some dedicated breeders were determined that their breeds should survive. Dr. Greig found that if she bred rabbits she could help to eke out the meat ration, and she was also able to sell the rabbit pelts.

Tibetan Terriers also helped some owners during the war, for their durable hair was sheared off and spun into wool to make clothing. A nucleus of Tibetan Terrier stock survived the war, and in 1947 Colonel Ronald Cardhew Duncan, author of the rare and precious little book *Tomu From Tibet*, imported his Princess Salli to England. A Nepalese official had presented Salli to Mrs. Duncan, and Salli spent two

Taikoo Kokonor was a lovely dog owned by Mr. R. C. Matthews of Victoria, BC, Canada. Circa 1931.

years in India where she produced a litter of puppies, one of which also came back to Britain with the Duncans.

THE 1950S

The Tibetan Terrier survived the war years and, in the 1950s, dog

---

> **THE TIBETAN TERRIER'S HOMELAND**
>
> The Tibetan Terrier's homeland, Tibet, is a high tableland, the plains around Lhasa about 2 miles above sea level. In size Tibet is equal to France, Germany and Great Britain combined, and temperatures vary considerably. Within the space of a day, temperature may range from below 0 to 100.4 degrees Fahrenheit.

showing again became a popular pastime, but the Tibetan Terrier was still not bountiful in number. Despite this, in 1956 it was decided that each of the Tibetan breeds, then under the auspices of the Tibetan Breeds Association, should form its own specialist breed club. The breed mustered the required number of 25 founder members and the Tibetan Terrier Club was founded.

In 1953 John and Constance Downey rescued a stray black dog that had allegedly jumped ship in Liverpool, having arrived from India, the country that had mis-named the Tibetan Terrier in the first place. They registered this male of dubious parentage with The Kennel Club, which later declared him a Tibetan Terrier. This dog, registered as Trojan

Miss Margaret Torrible was the owner of Kokonor kennels in Victoria, BC, Canada. She was the *only* breeder of Tibetan Terriers in North America in the early 1930s, and she receives much credit for making the breed known.

Shah of Ladkok was one of Mrs. Greig's Tibetan Terriers and was one of the most typical dogs in Britain during the early 1930s.

Ch. Shalimar's Polygor Flash, bred by Nina Wagner, winning a Best of Breed with handler Wendell Sammet.

by Miss H. Slaughter. Dawn and Dusky, naturally, became the Luneville foundation pair.

The Luneville Tibetans proved popular with the judges. This new line matured faster than the slow-developing Lamleh dogs and often beat them in the ring. After Dusky died, a Lamleh sire was used by the Luneville kennel, though this did not unite the two lines. On the contrary, the Downeys continued breeding their own dogs to one another, and their smaller, cuter Tibetans took over the British scene, casting the Lamleh dogs in the shadows. Today the Luneville dogs dominate the British show rings, and the Lamleh dogs are rarely seen. Of course, as we'll see, this would not be the Lamleh dogs fate in America.

ANOTHER BREED CLUB

The Tibetan Terrier Club seems not to have been sufficiently forward thinking, for by the 1960s there was a newer group of Tibetan Terrier enthusiasts who felt the existing club was rather uncommunicative. Therefore, in 1967, the Tibetan Terrier Association (TTA) was formed, the association's aims having been drawn up with very great care. Significantly, the aims encouraged "the careful keeping of Breeding Records" and "breeding in co-operation rather than in competition with one

Kynos and called "Dusky," became a champion and was mated with a bitch whose dam was also of unknown origin. This sketchy beginning formed the foundation of the very successful Luneville kennel.

Because Dr. Greig believed that Dusky was not pure-bred, her bitterness toward the Downeys and the Luneville line continued on and off until her death in 1972. Even so, a Lamleh bitch named "Dawn" was sold to the Downeys

another [to] work towards a secure future for the breed."

The truly remarkable number of 61 Tibetan Terriers attended the TTA's first breed show in September 1968, this judged by Herr Willy Pluss and Mme. Monique Stoecklin Pobe from Switzerland. The latter is a truly remarkable lady with whom the author has, in more recent years, had the pleasure of discussing the Tibetan breeds.

THE TIBETAN TERRIER COMES TO THE US

Gremlin Cortina, the first Tibetan Terrier to enter the United States, was sent by Dr. Greig of the famous Lamleh kennels in England in 1956 to Dr. and Mrs. Henry Murphy of Great Falls, Virginia. The second dog, a mate for "Girlie" (as Gremlin Cortina was known around the Murphys' home), was soon acquired from Dr. Greig; his name was "Gregory" or Kalai of Lamleh, the name which the Murphys decided to use as their kennel prefix. This foundation pair had its first litter of five puppies on March 31, 1957. In all, Dr. Greig sent 11 Tibetan Terriers to the Murphys over a 16-year period; she also sent 2 others to Mrs. Nell Hudson and Mrs. Miriam Shefler.

The first Luneville imports were Luneville Prince Kana and Luneville Princess Kim-Ba, imported by Mrs. Elizabeth

THE TT'S PARENT CLUB
Founded in 1957, the Tibetan Terrier Club of America (TTCA) actively promotes the interests of the breed, with a comprehensive code of ethics that must be adhered to by all its members. It holds national specialties over a few days to combine agility trials, obedience trials and conformation classes. This is a wonderful social event and includes an impressive black-tie dinner so that exhibitors can enjoy wearing all their finery. The TTCA also hosts educational and breeder seminars, and it has a Judges' Education Committee with a list of judges' mentors covering various different states. The Mount Vernon Tibetan Terrier Club, Inc. covers the District of Columbia, and the Bay Colony Tibetan Terrier Club covers Massachusetts.

Cammarata of St. Louis, Missouri in 1960 and 1965, respectively. Of the first 29 Tibetan Terriers imported, all came from England with the exception of 1 dog from Sweden. About half of these dogs were used for breeding, though not all had any lasting influence on the breed. From Mrs. Yuichi Katoh, Alice Murphy acquired another bitch named Nin-Ty of Lamleh, who produced well for her line. Imported in 1957, Shanak of Lamleh was one of the most important sires for the Kalai kennels and the American TT

Ch. Ashante Ashley of Bootiff, a Top Ten Tibetan Terrier of 1988 and the Westminster Breed winner in 1989.

board member until her death in 1976. After Mrs. Murphy's death, her Lamleh of Kalai breeding program was inherited by Jocelyn Therrell, who continued Mrs. Murphy's important line and bred a number of champions and top producers of her own.

Mrs. Ruth Hanson of California came into the breed in 1959 with the purchase of Kenspa Ponya Lamleh of Kalai and then Bozan-Ba Metog Lamleh of Kalai in 1960. Although Mrs. Hanson bred only a few litters and did not show dogs, she did much to promote the shaggy dog on the West Coast. Mr. and Mrs. James McDonald of Washington State did show their two bitches, Mee-Tu Lamleh of Kalai and Bo-Mo Yon Lamleh of Kalai in the early 1960s when the breed was in the AKC Miscellaneous Class. The McDonalds were hooked on the breed and Tibetan culture, extensively showing their dogs, acquiring English imports and breeding their own litters. They remained active showing TTs until 1972, even though their love for "all things Tibet" continued to blossom.

Mrs. Miriam Shefler of Connecticut was determined to become a breeder and after a few false starts bred her first litter with two dogs she purchased from Mrs. Murphy. Her Firetown Tibetans were shown in the Northeast, though none of these dogs had any lasting impact on the breed.

The Pine Valley kennels of Mrs. Barbara Harmon (Smith) and her

world, having produced 69 puppies in 13 breedings. One of his greatest offspring was Sen-Ge Snyin Lamleh of Kalai. One of the breed's top sires, Pai Cah of Lamleh, imported in 1958, and the bitch Bo-Sa of Lamleh also played important roles in producing at Kalai. The Kalai Tibetan Terriers had a lasting influence on nearly every early American kennel of Tibetan Terriers.

Largely due to Mrs. Murphy, the Tibetan Terrier Club of America came into being in 1957, and a registrar was set up. Mrs. Nell Hudson and then Mr. and Mrs. Julian Ross kept the breed registrations until the AKC took over in 1974. The breed entered the AKC Miscellaneous Class in 1963, where it would remain until 1973. Alice Murphy served as its first president, an office she kept until 1974; she remained a daughter Nancy produced some excellent stock in their 17 years in the breed. Even though they retired in the late 1970s, the Pine Valley dogs can be still found in pedigrees today.

Mr. and Mrs. Joseph Cammarata of St. Louis came into Tibetans in the early years, too, having acquired dogs directly from the Murphys. Their first litter (from Faith Lamleh of Kalai and Kalyani of Lamleh) arrived in 1960 to officially begin their Kalyani kennels. Elizabeth Cammarata acquired Luneville Prince Kana and then Luneville Princess Kim-Ba from the famous English kennel; Luneville Princess Posa arrived later, though she was sold later to Joan Rinker. Though active for a short while, this St. Louis family inspired other breeders in the Midwest to jump onto the Tibetan bandwagon, including Tom and Shirley Dickerson of Missouri.

The Dickersons started their Kyirong kennels with Zim Zim Lamleh of Kalai in 1963, whom they acquired from the Cammaratas. Zim Zim began the kennel with three excellent litters. One of her pups, Kalyani's Kala Yami of Kyirong, went to Dr. and Mrs. Francis Corcoran and was the first TT with an obedience title. Within a few years, the Dickersons acquired Kamba Kim-Bu of Shahi Taj and Luneville Princess Kim-Ba, the latter from

the Cammaratas. The Kamshe kennels of Don and Beverly Kammerer began with two of the Dickersons' progeny, Kyirong's Yiddu Sema Kimba and Kyirong's Dnar-ba Byin. The Kyirong kennels flourished for years, producing top-winning TTs like Ch. Tafra's Maha Kyo-Ga of Kyirong and later Ch. Kyirong's Shadrach of Camelot. The name "Tafra" refers to two TT fanciers, Tony and Kathy Tafra, who were satellite (and first-time) breeders for Kyirong when they produced

One of many BIS wins for Ch. Kyirong's Shadrach of Camelot, the number-one Tibetan Terrier in 1980–1983, handled by Walter Greene, winning under judge Al Treen.

CHAIN O' LAKES KENNEL CLUB JUNE 15 1980 BEST IN SHOW JUDGE MR ALFRED E TREEN

BEST IN SHOW

this amazing puppy who became an important sire for the breed.

From the Dickersons, Frank and Fran Corcoran acquired Kalyani's Kala Yami of Kyirong, out of Zim Zim, in the 1960s, but they didn't become active breeders until the mid-70s. Their Legs-Pa dogs, based in part on the imported Luneville Chubitang Kangri, CDX, were shown sparingly but did some nice winning in both conformation and obedience.

William Walsh entered the TT world in the early 1960s with some excellent dogs, Nor-Bu Lamleh of Kalai, Luneville Princess Posa, Kalyani's Kim and Jin-Da Malenki of Shahi-Taj. Princess Posa, of all the Luneville imports, ranks as one of the most influential Luneville dogs to come to the US. Walsh showed his own dogs, groomed them meticulously for the ring and bred a number of excellent dogs, including Ch. Tsa Lhor of Shahi-Taj, the foundation stud for Ed and Eileen Wilk's

In its fifth decade of lineage, here's the 2000 Westminster Breed winner bearing Anne Keleman's kennel prefix: Ch. Ti Song Ki Mik Blazing Sky.

program. Walsh's male dog Ch. Kyim's Tsabo of Shahi-Taj was sold to Joan Rinker as the foundation for her Loki kennels. He also sold Tehdeh Phurba of Shahi-Taj to Sue Mechem of Pennsylvania, who began her Katmandu TTs in 1968; this stud dog ("Teddy") became an important force in the breed, producing among other dogs Ch. Loki's Lady Luck, the foundation dam for Loki.

Kalyani's Kim, a male, by the way, sired the breed's first AKC champion named "Pirate," a boy with his namesake black patch over one eye (Pirate was known as "Pi" for short, though not mathematically, and officially Ch. Zim Sha's Tasha Ti Song), for Anne Keleman of northern California. Pi was Miss Keleman's first TT, whom she campaigned heavily in the media and at shows, hooking her, and most of the West Coast, on the breed. (Pi would become not only the breed's first AKC champion but also the first Group-placing TT.) In 1968 Miss Keleman produced her first litter, sired by Pi, out of her bitch Dirona's Jamel, this being the genesis of her well-known Ti Song Tibetans. Also used in Miss Keleman's program were Lamleh-Luneville combinations like Lhamoi Sister Lottie (bred by Linda T. Hope of England) and Ch. Chubitang's Toga of Legs-Pa (bred by the Corcorans). One of Ti Song's mostt famous dogs is

Eng./Am./Can. Ch. Ryttergarden's ChoCho, a Danish-bred dog who was shown in the UK by Anne Matthews and then sold to Miss Keleman. In the US, he became a top winner and an important producer, siring specialty winner Ch. Ti Song's J.P. Morgan of Tibeter among others. After over three decades in the breed, Miss Keleman retired from showing and breeding and today is regarded by the fancy as the "Mother Teresa of Tibetans," a title she cherishes. Looking back, she considers Ch. Ti Song's Mr. Personality her favorite Tibetan because his lively personality made him such a darling. "Persi" did much to convert Tibetan lovers from coast to coast, not the least of whom was breeder David Murray who holds the current record for most Best in Show wins with a Tibetan Terrier.

In 1971 Ed and Eileen Wilk started out with Ch. Lu-Rog's Georgina Pan-Dan Lha-Mo, CD ROM, who became a top brood bitch and was acquired from Beverly Luecke, and Granlee's Honey Kongjo, acquired from Sue Love. These two were combined with Ch. Tsa-Lhor of Shahi-Taj, the male from Bill Walsh, to set their Kontan kennels in motion. Ch. Tsa-Lhor of Shahi-Taj became the top TT in 1974, and he was followed by Ch. Kontan's Adam Bu-Tsa Lhor, the top TT in 1975, and Ch. Kontan's Shazam Bu-Tsa

Lhor, the breed's first BIS winner in the US and the top TT from 1976-1978.

Although there were many more Lamleh dogs imported, the Luneville dogs had a lasting effect too. As Luneville Princess Posa was an influential Luneville bitch in the States, Luneville Prince

America's first champion, say hello to "Pi," formally Ch. Zim Sha's Tasha Ti Song, owned by Anne Keleman and bred by Mrs. Neal Armond.

Anne Keleman's favorite TT won many fans for the breed with his bubbly personality and bouncy ways. This is "Persi," known in the show ring as Ch. Ti Song's Mr. Personality.

Kumana was the Luneville sire with the most impact here. Lamleh-Luneville crosses did not count for many influential Tibetans, though Mrs. Kathay Erceg's foundation dog Yak, formally Chi Chong of Kaims, and Alice and Bill Smith's Ch. Dokham Prin-Su's Caspar are two notable exceptions.

Actually, the Smiths' foundation dam also came from Lamleh and Luneville lines, Chubitang's Susan, whom they bred several times to Luneville Prince Kumana to establish their Prin-Su kennels in Ipswich, Massachusetts in

1967. The next import to come to Prin-Su kennels was Ch. Dokham Prin-Su's Caspar, ROM, who had Lamleh lines behind him, too. The Smiths have helped many Tibetan breeders along the way.

A litter for the record books, in 1970 Alice Murphy bred Yser-Bu Mo Lamleh of Kalai to Senge-Snyin Lamleh of Kalai and produced four puppies. Three of this fantastic foursome went on to be foundation stock for important kennels. Robert and Dorthe Chase of California based their Kyi-Ra kennels on one puppy who became Ch. Rem-Pa Gan-Zag Lamleh of Kalai, known to all as "Samson," who sired over 21 champions. Samson was bred to Se-Ma Lamleh of Kalai, Ch. Nettles Candace Lee and Ch. Tashi Tzu Chui of Angood to establish a West-Coast dynasty. Charles and Ruth Tevis named their Karchen kennel for a puppy who would shine as Ch. Karchen Lamleh of Kalai, appropriately known as "Star."

George and Jane Reif of Connecticut founded their Shaggar kennel on the third fantastic puppy whom they named Jai Zim Po Spod Lamleh of Kalai, the producer of many champions, not the least of whom was Ch. Shaggar Zemi Chumbi, the sire of 25 champions. The Reifs imported dogs directly from Dr. Greig before her death, including Topsai of Lamleh and

Ch. Legspa Summer Dream, a Top Ten Tibetan Terrier of 1984, winning Group First under judge Tom Stevenson.

Beauty of Lamleh, the latter becoming a Register of Merit dam. It's important to note that Jane Reif continues to be a force in this breed, not only through her important line of Tibetan Terriers but also through her books and articles on the breed. *The Tibetan Terrier Book*, privately published, offers the most complete history of the breed in the US and includes many historical photographs.

In 1972 Mr. and Mrs. James Jessup of Virginia imported their stud dog Ch. Lamleh Naihon directly from Dr. Greig's kennel. "Qhece," as he was known, sired a number of champions during the 1970s and early 1980s.

The Lost Creek Tibetan Terrier kennel of Nancy J. Van Cura began in 1973 with Am./Can. Ch. Serras Koko Nor of Lost Creek, Am./Can. Ch. Serras Sikang of Lost Creek, both of whom came from the Dickersons' breeding, and Ch. Kyirong Zim-Zim Na Lost Creek. Lost Creek produced no fewer than 37 champions in their decades in the breed.

On October 3, 1973, the Tibetan Terrier entered the Non-Sporting Group of the American Kennel Club. As we've noted, the first TT to become a champion was Zim Sha's Tasha Ti Song (the patched-eye "Pi"), owned by Anne Keleman and bred by Mrs. Neal Armond. The first bitch champion was Ch. Ma-Tasha

EST OF
D OR VARIETY
TONSVILLE
NEL CLUB
CTOBER
1988
JOHN ASHBEY

Missi Kim, also bred by Miss Keleman and owned by Arloine and Sue Bradshaw. The first British import to become an AKC champion was Ch. Dokham Prin-Su's Caspar, ROM, owned by the Smiths. Among the breeders and owners of the country's first champions, in addition to the above, were William Walsh, Judith Scheig, Mr. and Mrs. Robert Burton, Beverly Luecke, Marlene (Berch) Wolksy and Ed and Eileen Wilk. The first BOB winner at the Westminster Kennel Club Dog Show (1974) was Ch. Kontan's Adam Bu-Tsa Lhor, bred by the Wilks. The judge on this auspicious occasion was the

One of many great TTs bearing the Camelot prefix, this is Ch. Camelot's Knight of Sir Tyler, the Westminster Breed winner in 1988.

TOP BIS TIBETAN
The top Tibetan of all time, with over a hundred Best in Show wins, is Ch. Kimiks Bare Necessity, who won the Group at Westminster in 2005, the only Tibetan Terrier ever to have done so at this show. Bare Necessity is owned by Nikki Demers and was co-bred in partnership with Sheryl Rutledge-Schultis.

famous all-rounder Melbourne Downing. Later that year, Ch. Tsa Lhor of Shahi Taj, bred by Michael Walsh, was the first TT to win Group One. Lhor was shown by Susan Fisher. This was quite a feat, since the flashy show-stopping Bichon Frise also entered the Non-Sporting Group

just six months prior to the TT and was dominating the Group with its unique silhouette, glistening one coat and angelic charms.

The first TTCA specialty was held on October 8, 1978, and judge Edmund Sledzik selected Ch. Loki's Midnight Masquerade, bred by Joan Rinker, owner-handled by Donna Armstrong. As Loki's name indicates, he was a black dog, as was the Best of Opposite Sex that day, Ch. Mar-Lace's Chelsea of Ken-ba, bred by Marlene Berch and co-owned with Susan Reed.

On March 17, 1976, all of the Irish breeds mourned as Ch. Kontan's Shazam Bu-Tsa Lhor became the first Tibetan Terrier to win a Best in Show in the US. Bred by the Wilks and handled by Robert Fisher, Shazam was only 20 months of age, and the judge was Miss Anna Katherine Nicholas. Steve Furman's Ch. Kontan's Kori-Nor Bu-Tsa Lhor, bred by the Wilks, became the breed's first owner-handled Best in Show winner.

Among the top dogs from the first decade of the breed's AKC recognition were: Ch. Kyirong's Shadrach of Camelot, the top TT from 1980–1983, owned by Ron and Marie Smizinski and bred by the Dickersons; Ch. Tikon's Velvet Touch, bred and owned by Sam and Jo Pollock, both of these dogs multiple BIS winners; Ch. Kyim's

Tsabo of Shahi-Taj, bred by Bill Walsh and owned by Joan Rinker; Ch. Shaggar Zemi Chumbi, bred and owned by the Reifs; and Ch. Rem-Pa Gan-Zag Lamleh of Kalai, bred by Mrs. Murphy and owned by the Chases.

The top Tibetan Terrier breeder in America, Angelee Fargo's Charisma kennels came on the scene in the late 1970s and stayed active in the breed into the 1990s. Charisma kennels boasts dozens of top winners and producers, including Ch. Regalia's Goody Goody Our Gang, the dam of 24 champions, Charisma's Passionella, the dam of 18 champions, and Ch. Charisma's Dear Dagmar, the dam of 12 champions. Mrs. Fargo's stud dog, Ch. Marimark's Patches of Ti Song, the number-one TT in 1979, sired 14 champions. Ch. Charisma's Rube Begonia was the top TT in 1986, and Ch. Charisma Tiger Rag of Camelot, owned by Ron and Marie Smizinskis (Camelot), was the top dog in 1987. Ch. Charisma's Olive Oil and Ch. Charisma's Rainy Day Dreamer are other top winners. By 1990 Charisma had 89 champions to its credit.

Other top kennels in the breed include Gary and Susan Carr's Salishan, Gerald and Jeanette Chaix and Bob Carder's Regalia, Nina Wagner's Shalimar, Larry Schultis and Sheryl Rutledge-Schultis's Atisha, Dennis Gunshner's Kiara, Paul and Winnie Wuesthoff's Su-Khyi, Ron and Marie Smizinski's Camelot, Patricia Bernardo's Barnstorm, David Murray's Player, Laurel MacMinn's Sin-Pa, James Joseph and Linda Immell's Excaliber, Robert and Margaret Pankiewicz's Malishar and Robert and Jean Helton's Ka-Ba. The Salishan kennels produced top brood bitches, such as Ch. Kyi-Ra Ta-Ma-La of Salishan and Ch. Salishan Tessie Tukra, each the dam of 13 champions. Regalia kennels owned top sire Sunwind's Solar Eclipse, the sire of over a hundred champions. Ch. Karamain Ramadin Dali-Pa, owned by Bill and Sandy Hoffman and bred by Tuula Plathan, was the top TT from 1988-1990.

Ch. Tikon's Velvet Touch, bred and owned by Sam and Jo Pollock, the number-one Tibetan Terrier in 1984 and a multiple BIS winner.

TIBETAN WORLD CONGRESS

In 2003 America hosted the 8th Tibetan Terrier World Congress in Sturbridge, Massachusetts, and as always TT enthusiasts from all over the world attended the event to take part, with speakers from all the countries represented. For the US there were several speakers, each reporting on various areas of work carried out by the TTCA's Health Committee. The event was held in conjunction with the TTCA national specialty, with obedience, sweepstakes, breeders' showcase and of course regular classes with veterans and a parade of champions.

For the first time a representative from the Tibetan Terrier Club of Canada (TTCC) attended the World Congress. Despite the vastness of Canada, the national club is a small one, but remarkably 8 of the 48 members managed to get to this very special event. This enabled Penny White, TTCC president, to share with the rest of the Tibetan Terrier fraternity what was going on within the breed in Canada. Canadian Tibetan Terriers participate in all the traditional activities, conformation, obedience and agility, and they also earn Canine Good Citizen® Certificates and do therapy work. The TTCC supports the TTCA health and research initiatives, such as the DNA Blood Bank, to which most members have donated samples. In health matters, the Canadian TT owners tend to use the American registries for eyes, hips and hearing.

AMERICAN INFLUENCE ON BRITAIN

America has exported two highly important Tibetan Terriers to the UK during the last 15 years. Ch. Sukhi Kang Rimpoche, bred by Winnie Westerhoff, turned out to be the first Lamleh dog in 20 years to gain his championship title in the UK. This dog was pure American Lamleh and has had an influence on the breed in Britain, becoming the sire of several English champions, among them Ch. Araki Hank The Yank, who is one of only five Tibetan Terrier all-breed Best in Show winners to date.

Another influential American Tibetan Terrier that went to Britain was Ch. Atisha Star Ship Regalia, imported by Ken Sinclair of the famous Araki kennels and bred by Sheryl Rutledge and Jeanette Cox. He was sired by Ch. Sunwind Solar Eclipse, a top American stud dog, with well over a hundred champion offspring.

Perhaps the most influential US influence on the breed in the UK is Ch. Atisha's Passion For Magic who arrived in Britain in whelp to Ch. Atisha's Mark of Excellence. When the puppies, born in quarantine, were six weeks old, their dam was flown back to the States, and from this litter three gained their English championship titles. These were Chs. Araki American Way, Araki American Love and Araki All American Boy, who was Britain's youngest Group-winning Tibetan

Terrier at a Championship Show, at just over 12 months of age. This American-bred champion, whelped in the UK, has had great influence on the breed throughout the world.

The Atisha kennel is indeed one of the most influential in America with champions in many different countries. Ch. Araki Ari Kari of Kybo, bred in the UK and sired by Ch. Araki All American Boy, became a champion. He is one of the top stud dogs in the US and has had a wide influence on the breed. Ch. Atisha's Olympic Gold took Best in Show at the show held in conjunction with Tibetan Terrier World Congress.

TIBETAN TERRIERS AROUND THE WORLD

Dr. Greig sent a Tibetan Terrier bitch to Holland in 1931 and another a few years later, though it is not believed that these dogs lie behind the stock known in Holland today. Dr. Greig sent a Tibetan Terrier to Italy in 1937, and two of the Greigs' dogs went to Germany in 1939, where the same owner acquired a Tibetan import via Italy. Sadly this kennel came to a tragic end when its owner was shot in 1944.

The Greigs also sent a breeding pair to Denmark in 1939, but here the breed did not really become established until the 1960s. Sweden's Tibetan Terrier Club was formed in 1972, and enthusiasm for and dedication to the breed in

One of Britain's top breeders, Ken Sinclair of the famous Araki kennels, shown handling one of his fine Tibetans.

Scandinavia are very strong.

This author is greatly involved with Tibetan breeds and must comment on the sincere dedication of Tibetan Terrier breeders throughout the world. Every year foreign enthusiasts visit Crufts to watch the judging and to meet like-minded breeders, and Tibetan Terrier World Congresses are held on a biannual basis. These are held in different countries, and it is quite remarkable how well supported they are, with owners and enthusiasts traveling thousands of miles to attend. Undoubtedly, the Tibetan Terrier breed is in good hands, and those early exponents of the breed would surely be proud.

TIBETAN TERRIER

The Tibetan Terrier is a thoroughly enchanting breed in so very many ways. Indeed, it would be difficult not to be attracted to this delightful dog whose ancestors came from a land steeped in mystery. All the main characteristics of the Tibetan Terrier are related to function; they are not purely esthetic but vital to survival.

Size is manageable, neither too large nor too small, and the personality, coupled with intelligence, makes the breed a wonderful companion, one that is full of fun. It must be recognized from the outset, however, that the coat demands work to maintain it in tangle-free good condition.

Steeped in lure and mysticism, the Tibetan Terrier cannot fail to delight his fans with his jovial personality and effervescent sense of fun.

PERSONALITY

Lively and good-natured, the Tibetan Terrier is a thoroughly loyal companion dog, though one should appreciate that the breed is meant to be sparing of affection to strangers.

Because of the breed's liveliness and intelligence, the Tibetan Terrier needs firm but gentle handling. From puppyhood it must be trained to know that its owner is the boss, and then the owner will be rewarded with both loyalty and devotion. Although the Tibetan Terrier is both determined and game, it should by no means be ferocious.

DOUBLE DEWCLAWS

Dewclaws on the Tibetan Terrier are frequently removed by breeders when puppies are three days old. This prevents accidental tearing and makes grooming easier. Occasionally, double dewclaws are present on the hind feet. If dewclaws are allowed to remain, they must be checked frequently and will need to be clipped.

PHYSICAL CHARACTERISTICS

Constructed with purpose and strength, this is a sturdy, robust dog of medium size, instantly recognizable as an Oriental breed because of its square outline and long coat. The Tibetan Terrier is an unexaggerated breed in all respects, with a medium length of skull and a body that is well muscled, compact and powerful. The long hind legs, with their well-bent stifles, are designed to help this special breed thrive at high altitudes on difficult terrain, to which the breed has historically been accustomed.

The feet are large, round and flat, such that they can be used not only to grip well but also to serve as "snowshoes" in the breed's homeland of Tibet. No arch in the foot should be apparent, and the Tibetan Terrier stands well down on its pads, emphasizing the flat look of the feet. The pads are thick, and there is hair growth between them.

SIZE

Size of the Tibetan Terrier is something that causes debate, as it does seem to vary quite considerably. According to the American Kennel Club breed standard, males should be 15–16 inches at shoulder, and bitches slightly smaller. However, the original Tibetan Breeds Association standard, drawn up in 1934, gave 17 inches as a maximum height

The author meets two Tibetan Terriers and a Buddhist nun in the Himalayan Mountains. The puppy in the author's hands was sired by the dog shown in this photo.

and was only reduced as the result of a printing error during those early years.

The disparity in size stems from the breed in its homeland, where dogs living in the most severe climatic conditions needed to be larger than others in order to adequately perform their functions in life. Not all Tibetan Terriers fall within the official height range, but quality and balance should be regarded as more important than size.

Although the British/FCI (Fédération Cynologique Internationale) standard gives no indication of weight, the AKC standard sets the average weight range at 20–24 lb, but indicates a wider range of 18–30 lb. As a general guide, a Tibetan Terrier at the lower end of the height scale may weigh about 18–20 lb, whereas a dog around 16 inches is likely to weigh 25–30 lb.

COAT AND COLORS

The Tibetan Terrier possesses a double coat: a fine, woolly undercoat and a long, profuse topcoat. Such a coat would have been necessary for the breed to survive in its homeland, a country with such extreme weather conditions. For such survival, the topcoat needs to be durable and waterproof to prevent the dog's undercoat from becoming wet. It is described as "fine" (meaning that it should not be coarse) and should never be silky or woolly, according to the breed standard. The long coat of the Tibetan Terrier does not

Bitches are slightly smaller than male dogs.

reach to the ground as does the coat of the modern-day Lhasa Apso, but development of coat within the breed does seem to vary with different breeding lines. It may be straight or waved, but should never be curly.

A Tibetan Terrier's adult coat does not fully appear until well over one year of age, and sometimes the coat does not reach maturity until even three or four years. A puppy's coat is softer and often has no undercoat, this developing during adolescence.

The breed's long double coat does require a substantial amount of grooming if it is to be kept tangle-free and in good order. This is a very serious point to be considered before deciding to bring a Tibetan Terrier into your home. On the more positive side, because the coat has a tendency to mat, it does not shed very much; instead, the dead hair is taken out during the grooming process.

To stand quietly and watch a show ring full of well-groomed Tibetan Terriers, in a wealth of colors, is a veritable feast for the eye. Their colors vary considerably, perhaps more so than most other breeds, and the AKC standard accepts all colors and combinations.

The British breed standard, which is more specific here, allows for the following colors: white, golden, cream, gray or smoke, black, parti-color and tricolors.

It does not allow for liver or chocolate colors, though these colors do exist in the breed and make very attractive pets. Interestingly, the Tibetan people themselves seem not to have any objection to liver- and chocolate-colored dogs.

Coat color has a bearing on skin pigment, and dogs that are liver and chocolate have a genetic make-up that does not allow them to have the desired black nose and black eye rims. Parti-colored and tricolored dogs have coats made up from more than one color.

TAILS

In common with other Tibetan breeds, the Tibetan Terrier's tail is set on high and carried over the back. The tail is effectively an extension of the spine and is an important means of expression. In this breed it should always be carried in a gay curl. Towards the tip of the tail there may be a kink, which is perfectly correct, though not essential. Owners must never try to straighten out this kink, as that would cause injury. The kink is a highly typical feature found on many Tibetan dogs.

HEALTH CONSIDERATIONS

The Tibetan Terrier is generally a hardy dog, and dedicated breeders have conscientiously striven to seek out and work toward elimination of hereditary problems in the breed. In this way such problems

A dark draft, anyone? This black Tibetan Terrier is named Guinness, hence the sweatshirt.

can be monitored and corrective measures taken, breeding programs being altered or curtailed according to need. All credit is due to those who have worked so hard for the betterment of the breed.

Various health-testing programs are now available, and owners should take guidance from their country's Tibetan Terrier breed clubs as to which tests are mandatory or advisable. Contact

---

SHIELDING THE EYES

The Tibetan Terrier's hair falls forward over the eyes. In the harsh environment of Tibet, this enables the hair to shield the eyes from the bright sunlight, whiteness of the snow and torrents of dust.

GOOD LUCK CHARM
The Tibetan Terrier was believed to bring good luck to its owner, so in their homeland they were never sold, for it would have been tempting fate if one were to sell one's "luck."

breeding. This helps those closely involved with the Tibetan Terrier to build up a genetic picture of the breed, thereby helping them in their endeavors to eliminate health problems.

PROGRESSIVE RETINAL ATROPHY
Progressive retinal atrophy, usually referred to as PRA, is an inherited problem that was officially recognized in the breed some years ago. Thanks to efficient testing, cases of PRA in this breed now occur only rarely. The form of PRA that can affect the Tibetan Terrier is GPRA (generalized PRA).

GPRA is an eye disorder, not usually discovered until adulthood, in which a dog progressively goes blind. This is often first noticed by night-blindness, but total blindness is unfortunately the inevitable end result. Thankfully, there is no pain. It is essential that both the sire and dam of a litter are eye-tested prior to mating, and breeders have to use their knowledge of hereditary factors to avoid, if possible, doubling up on the gene which carries this inherited disease.

addresses of specialist clubs are usually available through the American Kennel Club.

All Tibetan Terriers used for breeding must be tested for eye disorders. However, pet owners interested in playing their part in benefiting the long-term health of the breed should also seriously consider having health checks, even though they may have no plans to use their dogs for

PRIMARY LENS LUXATION
Lens luxation causes extreme pain and comes about when the lens of the eye becomes displaced from its usual position, which should be behind the iris. This creates a rise of pressure in the eye and ultimately blindness unfortunately results.

HIP DYSPLASIA

Hip dysplasia occurs in many breeds and is a problem involving the ball and socket joint at the hip. It is a developmental condition caused by the interaction of many genes. This results in looseness of the hip joints, and although not always painful, it can cause lameness and typical movement can be impaired.

Although a dog's environment does not actually cause hip dysplasia, this may have some bearing on how unstable the hip joint eventually becomes. Osteoarthritis eventually develops as a result of the instability. Tests for hip dysplasia are available. Both hips are tested and scored individually; the lower the score the less the degree of dysplasia. Clearly dogs with high scores should not be incorporated in breeding programs.

PATELLAR LUXATION

Some Tibetan Terriers have been known to suffer from patellar

luxation, a substandard formation of the knee joint. Several of these cases have been only mild, though others have been both painful and disabling. Sometimes it is necessary to resort to surgery, but understandably, any dog seriously affected should not be bred from.

For easy coat management by their owners, these Tibetan Terriers are trimmed short in what is popularly called the pet trim.

The Tibetan's manageable size, intelligence and loyalty make it a very viable breed for assistance work.

> **BE KIND TO ANIMALS**
> His Holiness the Dalai Lama, now living in exile in Dharamsala in Northern India, owned a Tibetan Terrier by the name of "Senge." All true Buddhists are kind to their dogs, as they are to all animals. They believe in reincarnation, meaning that any animal, even a lowly ant, might at one time have been a human relation.

TIBETAN TERRIER

INTRODUCTION
TO THE BREED STANDARD

The breed standard for the Tibetan Terrier is set down by the American Kennel Club and revised only occasionally, usually with some guidance from experienced people within the breed clubs, although the American Kennel Club has the final word as to what is incorporated and in what manner.

However, a club may approach the American Kennel Club to request revision of the standard if the membership feels this is necessary, as has recently been the case regarding the lack of any reference to the Tibetan Terrier's neck.

A breed standard is designed effectively to paint a picture in words, though each reader will almost certainly have a slightly

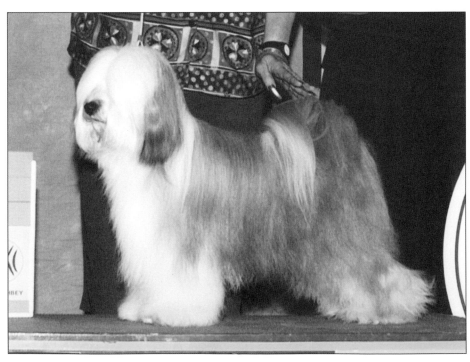

An excellent example of a sound, well-coated Tibetan Terrier, this is Ch. Excalibur's Sticks N Stones, a Best in Show-winning dog.

different way of interpreting these words. But to fully comprehend the intricacies of a breed, reading words alone is never enough. In addition, it is essential for devotees to watch other Tibetan Terriers being judged at shows and, if possible, to attend specialist breed seminars. This enables owners to absorb as much as possible about the breed they love.

In Britain, the Tibetan Terrier breed clubs also hold training sessions for judges, leading toward judging examinations. This ensures that those wishing to progress

Ch. Barnstorm's Ann of Ivy Gables, was the number-one Tibetan Terrier in 2000 and a multiple BIS winner.

further in the breed fully understand every aspect of the breed so that they are better equipped to judge when the opportunity presents itself.

The opening section of each standard is headed, "General Appearance." This gives a short précis of what the breed should look like. From this opening sentence, one can see immediately that a typical Tibetan Terrier should be sturdy and medium-sized, long-haired and with an outline that is generally square. We also read that the breed has a resolute expression. So it takes little comprehension to realize immediately that a Tibetan Terrier with a long back, somewhat resembling a toy breed in bone structure and size, and with a short coat, would be thoroughly untypical of the breed.

FOR THE LOVE OF DOGS

Breeding involves a major financial investment, but just as important is your investment in time. You'll spend countless hours in caring for, cleaning (and cleaning up after), feeding and training the litter. Furthermore, we haven't yet mentioned the strain and health risks that delivering a litter pose to the dam. Many bitches die in puppybirth, and that is a very high price to pay. Experienced breeders, with established lines and reputations in the field, are not in the hobby for financial gain. Those "breeders" who are in it for profit are not true breeders at all and are not reputable sources from which to buy puppies. Remember, there is nothing more to breeding dogs than the love of the dogs.

The Tibetan Terrier's breed standard is almost unique in that it permits either a scissors or a reverse scissors bite, meaning that the upper teeth closely overlap the lower ones, or the other way around. Undoubtedly the majority of Tibetan Terriers have scissors bites, but a reverse scissors bite is not to be penalized, and it is important that judges not so familiar with the breed fully understand this.

However familiar one is with the breed, it is always worth refreshing one's memory by re-reading the standard, for it is sometimes all too easy to overlook, or perhaps conveniently forget, certain

Head study showing correct type, structure, proportion and a mature coat.

features. The breed standard undoubtedly helps breeders to breed stock that comes as close to the standard as possible and helps judges to know exactly what they are looking for in finding as typical a Tibetan Terrier as possible to head their line of winners.

THE AMERICAN KENNEL CLUB BREED STANDARD FOR THE TIBETAN TERRIER

The Tibetan Terrier evolved over many centuries, surviving in Tibet's extreme climate and difficult terrain. The breed developed a protective double coat, compact size, unique foot construction and great agility. The Tibetan Terrier served as a steadfast, devoted companion in all of his owner's endeavors.

General Appearance

The Tibetan Terrier is a medium-sized dog, profusely coated, of powerful build, and square in proportion. A fall of hair covers the eyes and foreface. The well-feathered tail curls up and falls forward over the back. The feet are large, flat, and round in shape producing a snowshoe effect that provides traction. The Tibetan Terrier is well balanced and capable of both strong and efficient movement. The Tibetan Terrier is shown as naturally as possible.

Tibetan Terrier in profile showing correct type, structure, balance and a mature coat.

Head

Skull—Medium length neither broad nor coarse. The length from the eye to the tip of the nose is equal to the length from eye to the occiput. The skull narrows slightly from ear to eye. It is not domed but not absolutely flat between the ears. The head is well furnished with long hair, falling forward over the eyes and foreface. The cheekbones are curved but not so overdeveloped as to bulge. *Muzzle*—The lower jaw has a small amount of beard. *Stop*—There is marked stop but not exaggerated. *Nose*—Black. *Teeth*—White, strong and evenly placed. There is a distinct curve in the jaws between the canines. A tight scissors bite, a tight reverse scissors bite or a level bite are equally acceptable. A slightly undershot bite is acceptable. *Eyes*—Large, set fairly wide

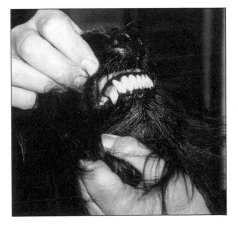

Quite unusual for a breed standard, there are four acceptable bites in the Tibetan Terrier: scissors, reverse scissors, level and slightly undershot.

CONFORMATION IN PROFILE

Short neck, upright shoulders, high in the rear, lacking angulation behind.

Long back, poor topline and low tailset.

Long back, low on leg, soft topline, low tailset and lacking angulation behind.

Outline of a dog under the coat showing correct structure proportion and tailset.

apart, dark brown and may appear black in color, neither prominent nor sunken. Eye rims are dark in color. *Ears*—Pendant, falling not too close to the head, heavily feathered with a "V" shaped leather proportionate to the head. *Faults*—Weak pointed muzzle. Any color other than a black nose. Overshot bite or a very undershot bite or a wry mouth. Long narrow head. Lack of fall over the eyes and foreface.

Neck and Body
Neck—Length proportionate to the body and head. *Body*—Compact, square and strong, capable of both speed and endurance. *Topline*—The back is level in motion. *Chest*—Heavily furnished. The brisket extends downward to the top of the elbow in the mature Tibetan Terrier. *Ribs*—The body is well ribbed up and never cloddy or coarse. The rib cage is not too wide across the chest and narrows slightly to permit the forelegs to work free at the sides. *Loin*—Slightly arched. *Tail*—Medium length, heavily furnished, set on fairly high and falls forward over the back, may curl to either side. There may be a kink near the tip.

Forequarters
Shoulders—Sloping, well muscled and well laid back.

Legs—Straight and strong when viewed from the front. Heavily furnished. The vertical distance from the withers to the elbow equals the distance from the elbows to the ground. *Feet*—The feet of the Tibetan Terrier are unique in form among dogs. They are large, flat, and round in shape producing a snowshoe effect that provides traction. The pads are thick and strong. They are heavily furnished with hair between the toes and pads. Hair between the toes and pads may be trimmed level with the underside of the pads for health reasons. The dog should stand well down on its pads. *Dewclaws*—May be removed.

Hindquarters
Legs—Well furnished, with well bent stifles and the hind legs are slightly longer than the forelegs. *Thighs*—Relatively broad and well muscled. *Hocks*—Low set and turn neither in nor out. *Feet*—Same as forefeet. Dewclaws May be removed.

Coat
Double coat. Undercoat is soft and woolly. Outer coat is profuse and fine but never silky or woolly. May be wavy or straight. Coat is long but should not hang to the ground. When standing on a hard surface an area of light should be seen under the dog. The coat of

Ch. RiLees White Diamonds Revark, the number-one Tibetan Terrier of 1999.

puppies is shorter, single and often has a softer texture than that of adults. A natural part is often present over the neck and back. *Fault*—Lack of double coat in adults. Sculpturing, scissoring, stripping or shaving are totally contrary to breed type and are serious faults.

Color
Any color or combination of colors including white are acceptable to the breed. There

Tibetan Terrier feet should be large, flat and with hair growing between the pads.

The Tibetan Terrier dog stands 15 to 16 inches, though the bitches are slightly smaller, though never below 14 inches.

are no preferred colors or combinations of colors.

Gait
The Tibetan Terrier has a free, effortless stride with good reach in front and flexibility in the rear allowing full extension. When gaiting the hind legs should go neither inside nor outside the front legs but should move on the same track approaching single tracking when the dog is moved at a fast trot. The dog with the correct foot and leg construction moves with elasticity and drive indicating that the dog is capable of great agility as well as endurance.

The desired movement of the Tibetan Terrier is characterized by a free and effortless stride. At a fast trot, the feet should move on the same track.

Size

Average weight is 20 to 24 pounds, but the weight range may be 18 to 30 pounds. Proportion of weight to height is far more important than specific weight and should reflect a well-balanced square dog. The average height in dogs is 15 to 16 inches, bitches slightly smaller. The length, measured from the point of shoulder to the root of tail, is equal to the height measured from the highest point of the

The AKC standard permits all colors and combinations, even this lovely chocolate. In the UK, this color is not permitted for exhibition.

withers to the ground. *Faults*— Any height above 17 inches or below 14 inches.

Temperament

The Tibetan Terrier is highly intelligent, sensitive, loyal, devoted and affectionate. The breed may be cautious or reserved. *Fault*—Extreme shyness.

Approved March 10, 1987

BETTER THAN THE AVERAGE DOG

Even though you may never show your dog, you should still read the breed standard. The breed standard tells you more than just physical specifications such as how tall your dog should be; it also describes how he should act, how he should move and what unique qualities make him the breed that he is. You are not investing money in a pure-bred dog so that you can own a dog that "sort of looks like" the breed you're purchasing. You want a typical, handsome representative of the breed, one that all of your friends and family and people you meet out in public will recognize as the breed you've so carefully selected and researched. If the parents of your prospective puppy bear little or no resemblance to the dog described in the breed standard, you should keep searching!

TIBETAN TERRIER

GROWING UP

The developmental rate of Tibetan Terriers differs considerably according to breeding lines. They will reach full height during puppyhood, but continue to develop bodily thereafter, some not maturing fully until three or four years of age.

HOW TO SELECT A PUPPY

Before deciding to look for a puppy, it is essential that you are fully clear in your mind that a Tibetan Terrier is the right breed for both you and your family. This is not an unduly large breed, so size should not present a major problem, but a Tibetan Terrier is lively and full of energy, so this should be borne in mind. You must also carefully consider whether or not you will be able to cope with the long double coat, not just now, but for the next 13 years or so.

You may also wish to give some consideration to coat color, although this should really be a low priority. Having said that, if you have really set your heart on a black Tibetan Terrier, it would perhaps be unwise to change your preference too rapidly, simply because another color is more readily available.

Something else to consider is whether or not to take out veterinary insurance. Vets' bills can mount up, and you must always be certain that sufficient funds are available to give your dog any veterinary attention that may be needed. Keep in mind, though, that routine vaccinations will not be covered by insurance policies.

Tibetan Terrier puppies almost invariably look enchanting, but you must select one from a caring breeder who has given the puppies all the attention they have deserved and has looked after them well.

If you visit a number of different kennels, you may well find that the puppies differ somewhat, as this is a breed that matures more or less rapidly according to breeding lines. Nonetheless, a young puppy should look well fed, but not pot bellied, as this might indicate worms. Take a note of eyes that should look bright and clear, without discharge. Nor, of course, should there be any discharge from the nose and certainly no evidence of loose bowels.

The puppy you choose should have a healthy-looking coat and a lively personality. Under no circumstances "take pity on" the weakling of the litter, nor on one that is unduly shy, nervous or aggressive.

SIGNS OF A HEALTHY PUPPY

Healthy puppies are robust little fellows who are alert and active, sporting shiny coats and supple skin. They should not appear lethargic, bloated or pot-bellied, nor should they have flaky skin or runny or crusted eyes or noses. Their stools should be firm and well formed, with no evidence of blood or mucus.

It is essential that you select a breeder with the utmost care. Initially, the American Kennel Club will be able to put you in contact with a breed club, or perhaps directly with breeders, but it is always a good idea to visit a large show at which Tibetan Terriers will be exhibited. This may be either an all-breed show or a specialty show, both of which will provide you with the chance to meet a good variety of breeders and their dogs.

A Tibetan Terrier puppy fairly corners the market on irresistible. Who can deny the lovable charm of this fuzzy baby?

A COMMITTED NEW OWNER

By now you should understand what makes the Tibetan Terrier a most unique and special dog, one that may fit nicely into your family and lifestyle. If you have researched breeders, you should be able to recognize a knowledge-able and responsible Tibetan Terrier breeder who cares not only about his pups but also about what kind of owner you will be. If you have completed the final step in your new journey, you have found a litter, or possibly two, of quality Tibetan Terrier pups.

A visit with the puppies and their breeder should be an education in itself. Breed research, breeder selection and puppy visitation are very

TEMPERAMENT ABOVE ALL ELSE

Regardless of breed, a puppy's disposition is perhaps his most important quality. It is, after all, what makes a puppy lovable and "livable." If the puppy's parents or grandparents are known to be snappy or aggressive, the puppy is likely to inherit those tendencies. That can lead to serious problems, such as the dog's becoming a biter, which can lead to eventual abandonment.

important aspects of finding the puppy of your dreams. Beyond that, these things also lay the foundation for a successful future with your pup. Puppy personali-ties within each litter vary, from the shy and easygoing puppy to the one who is dominant and assertive, with most pups falling somewhere in between. By spending time with the puppies you will be able to recognize certain behaviors and what these behaviors indicate about each pup's temperament. Which type of pup will complement your family dynamics is best determined by observing the puppies in action within their "pack." Your breeder's expertise and recommendations are also valuable. Although you may fall in love with a bold and brassy male, the breeder may suggest that another pup would be best

When visiting the breeder's kennel, you should have the opportunity to meet the dam of the puppies as well as some other relatives. It is a decided advantage if the breeder has the sire on premises as well.

Here's a handsome TT puppy ready to go to his new home... and he's got his own wheels.

for you. The breeder's experience in rearing Tibetan Terrier pups and matching their temperaments with appropriate humans offers the best assurance that your pup will meet your needs and expectations. The type of puppy that you select is just as important as your decision that the Tibetan Terrier is the breed for you.

CHOICE OF COLOR

While color variation in the Tibetan Terrier is mind-boggling, a litter usually only contains five puppies, and sometimes fewer colors. Though each pattern is eye-catching and lovely, you may have to find more than one litter to find the color on which you've set your heart.

The decision to live with a Tibetan Terrier is a serious commitment and not one to be taken lightly. This puppy is a living sentient being that will be dependent on you for basic survival for his entire life. Beyond the basics of survival— food, water, shelter and protection—he needs much, much more. The new pup needs love, nurturing and a proper canine education to mold him into a responsible, well-behaved canine citizen. Your Tibetan Terrier's health and good manners will need consistent monitoring and regular "tune-ups," so your job as a responsible dog owner will be ongoing throughout every stage of his life. If you are not prepared to accept these responsibilities and commit to them for the next

Food and water bowls of stainless steel are sturdy and easy to clean.

Being prepared for your puppy's arrival will make things easier for both of you.

decade, likely longer, then you are not prepared to own a dog of any breed.

Although the responsibilities of owning a dog may at times tax your patience, the joy of living with your Tibetan Terrier far outweighs the workload, and a well-mannered adult dog is worth your time and effort. Before your very eyes, your new charge will grow up to be your most loyal friend, devoted to you unconditionally.

YOUR TIBETAN TERRIER SHOPPING LIST

Just as expectant parents prepare a nursery for their baby, so should you ready your home for the arrival of your Tibetan Terrier pup. If you have the necessary puppy supplies purchased and in place before he comes home, it will ease the puppy's transition from the warmth and familiarity of his mom and littermates to the brand-new environment of his new home and human family. You will be too busy to stock up and prepare your house after your pup comes home, that's for sure!

Imagine how a pup must feel upon being transported to a strange new place. It's up to you to comfort him and to let your little pup know that he is going to be happy with you.

FOOD AND WATER BOWLS

Your puppy will need separate bowls for his food and water. Stainless steel pans are generally preferred over plastic bowls since they sterilize better and pups are less inclined to chew on the metal. Heavy-duty ceramic bowls are popular, but consider how often you will have to pick up those heavy bowls. Buy adult-sized pans, as your puppy will grow into them before you know it.

THE DOG CRATE

If you think that crates are tools of punishment and confinement for when a dog has misbehaved, think again. Most breeders and almost all trainers recommend a crate as the preferred house-training aid as well as for all-around puppy training and safety. Because dogs are natural den creatures that prefer cave-like environments, the benefits of crate use are many. The crate provides the puppy with his very own "safe house," a cozy place to sleep, take a break or seek comfort with a favorite toy; a travel aid to house your dog when on the road, at motels or at the vet's office; a training aid to help teach your puppy proper toileting habits; and a place of solitude when non-dog people happen to drop by and

Mesh crate on the left, wire crate on the right and fiberglass crate on top.

don't want a lively puppy—or even a well-behaved adult dog—saying hello or begging for attention.

Crates come in several types, although the wire crate and the fiberglass airline-type crate are the most popular. Both are safe and your puppy will adjust to either one, so the choice is up to you. The wire crates offer better visibility for the pup as well as better ventilation. Many of the wire crates easily collapse into suitcase-size carriers. The fiberglass crates, similar to those used by the airlines for animal transport, are sturdier and more den-like. However, the fiberglass crates do not collapse and are less ventilated than a wire crate, which can be problematic in hot weather. Some of the newer crates are made of heavy plastic mesh;

CRATE EXPECTATIONS

To make the crate more inviting to your puppy, you can offer his first meal or two inside the crate, always keeping the crate door open so that he does not feel confined. Keep a favorite toy or two in the crate for him to play with while inside. You can also cover the crate at night with a lightweight sheet to make it more den-like and remove the stimuli of household activity. Never put him into his crate as punishment or as you are scolding him, since he will then associate his crate with negative situations and avoid going there.

they are very lightweight and fold up into slim-line suitcases. However, a mesh crate might not be suitable for a pup with manic chewing habits.

Don't bother with a puppy-sized crate. Although your Tibetan Terrier will be a wee fellow when you bring him home, he will grow up in the blink of an eye and your puppy crate will be useless. Purchase a crate that will accommodate an adult Tibetan Terrier. He will stand about 15 to 16 inches when full grown, so a medium- to large-sized crate will fit him nicely.

BEDDING AND CRATE PADS
Your puppy will enjoy some type of soft bedding in his "room" (the crate), something he can snuggle

into to feel cozy and secure. Old towels or blankets are good choices for a young pup, since he may (and probably will) have a toileting accident or two in the crate or decide to chew on the bedding material. Once he is fully trained and out of the early chewing stage, you can replace the puppy bedding with a permanent crate pad if you prefer. Crate pads and other dog beds run the gamut from inexpensive to high-end doggie-designer styles, but don't splurge on the good stuff until you are sure that your puppy is reliable and won't tear it up or make a mess on it.

PUPPY TOYS
Just as infants and older children require objects to stimulate their minds and bodies, puppies need toys to entertain their curious brains, wiggly paws and achy

---

WHAT SIZE IS THE RIGHT SIZE?
When purchasing a crate, buy one that will fit an adult-size dog. Puppy crates are poor investments, since puppies quickly outgrow them. The crate should accommodate an adult dog in a standing position so that he has room to stand up, turn around and lie down comfortably. A larger crate is fine but not necessary for the dog's comfort, as most of his crate time will be spent lying down and napping.

teeth. A fun array of safe doggie toys will help satisfy your puppy's chewing instincts and distract him from gnawing on the leg of your antique chair or your new leather sofa. Most puppy toys are cute and look as if they would be a lot of fun, but not all are necessarily safe or good for your puppy, so use caution when you go puppy-toy shopping.

Although Tibetan Terriers are not known to be voracious chewers like many other dogs, they still love to chew. The best "chewcifiers" are nylon and hard rubber bones, which are safe to gnaw on and come in sizes appropriate for all age groups and breeds. Be especially careful of natural bones, which can splinter or develop dangerous sharp edges; pups can easily swallow or choke on those bone splinters.

Veterinarians often tell of surgical nightmares involving bits of splintered bone because in addition to the danger of choking, the sharp pieces can damage the intestinal tract.

Similarly, rawhide chews, while a favorite of most dogs and puppies, can be equally dangerous. Pieces of rawhide are easily swallowed after they get all soft and gummy from chewing, and dogs have been known to choke on large pieces of ingested rawhide. Rawhide chews should be offered only when you can supervise the puppy.

Soft woolly toys are special puppy favorites. They come in a wide variety of cute shapes and sizes; some look like little stuffed animals. Puppies love to shake them up and toss them about, or simply carry them around. Be careful of fuzzy toys that have button eyes or noses that your pup could chew off and swallow, and make sure that he does not

Puppies need toys just as much as children—and for the same reasons.

GOOD CHEWING

Chew toys run the gamut from rawhide chews to hard sterile bones and everything in between. Rawhides are all-time favorites, but they can cause choking when they become mushy from repeated chewing, causing them to break into small pieces that are easy to swallow. Rawhides are also highly indigestible, so many vets advise limiting rawhide treats. Hard sterile bones are great for plaque prevention as well as chewing satisfaction. Dispose of them when the ends become sharp or splintered.

TOYS 'R SAFE

The vast array of tantalizing puppy toys is staggering. Stroll through any pet shop or pet-supply outlet and you will see that the choices can be overwhelming. However, not all dog toys are safe or sensible. Most very young puppies enjoy soft woolly toys that they can snuggle with and carry around. (You know they have outgrown them when they shred them up!) Avoid toys that have buttons, tabs or other enhancements that can be chewed off and swallowed. Soft toys that squeak are fun, but make sure your puppy does not disembowel the toy and remove (and swallow) the squeaker. Toys that rattle or make noise can excite a puppy, but they present the same danger as the squeaky kind and so require supervision. Hard rubber toys that bounce can also entertain a pup, but make sure that the toy is too big for your pup to swallow.

disembowel a squeaky toy to remove the squeaker! Braided rope toys are similar in that they are fun to chew and toss around, but they shred easily and the strings are easy to swallow. The strings are not digestible and, if the puppy doesn't pass them in his stool, he could end up at the vet's office. As with rawhides, your puppy should be closely monitored with rope toys.

If you believe that your pup has ingested one of these forbidden objects, check his stool for the next couple of days to see if he passes them when he defecates. At the same time, also watch for signs of intestinal distress. A call to your veterinarian might be in order to get his advice and be on the safe side.

An all-time favorite toy for puppies (young and old!) is the empty gallon milk jug. Hard plastic juice containers—46 ounces or more—are also excellent. Such containers make lots of noise when they are batted about, and puppies go crazy with delight as they play with them. However, they don't often last very long, so be sure to remove and replace them when they get chewed up on the ends.

A word of caution about homemade toys: be careful with your choices of non-traditional play objects. Never use old shoes or socks, since a puppy cannot distinguish between the old ones on which he's allowed to chew and the new ones in your closet that are strictly off limits. That principle applies to anything that resembles something that you don't want your puppy to chew.

COLLARS

A lightweight nylon collar is the best choice for a very young pup. Quick-click collars are easy to put on and remove, and they can be adjusted as the puppy grows. Introduce him to his collar as soon as he comes home to get him accustomed to wearing it. He'll get used to it quickly and won't mind a bit. Make sure that it is snug enough that it won't slip off, yet loose enough to be comfortable for the pup. You should be able to slip two fingers

Your Tibetan Terrier puppy will need something to sink his teeth into; make sure that what you provide him with is safe.

between the collar and his neck. Check the collar often, as puppies grow in spurts, and his collar can become too tight almost overnight. Choke collars are for training purposes only and should never be used on a puppy under four or five months old.

LEASHES

A 6-foot nylon lead is an excellent choice for a young puppy. It is lightweight and not as tempting to chew as a leather lead. You can switch to a 6-foot leather lead after your pup has grown and is used to walking politely on a lead. For initial puppy walks and house-training purposes, you should invest in a shorter lead so that you have more control over the puppy. At

---

TEETHING TIME

All puppies chew. It's normal canine behavior. Chewing just plain feels good to a puppy, especially during the three- to five-month teething period when the adult teeth are breaking through the gums. Rather than attempting to eliminate such a strong natural chewing instinct, you will be more successful if you redirect it and teach your puppy what he may or may not chew. Correct inappropriate chewing with a sharp "No!" and offer him a chew toy, praising him when he takes it. Don't become discouraged. Chewing usually decreases after the adult teeth have come in.

COLLARING OUR CANINES

The standard flat collar with a buckle or a snap, in leather, nylon or cotton, is widely regarded as the everyday all-purpose collar. If the collar fits correctly, you should be able to fit two fingers between the collar and the dog's neck.

Leather Buckle Collars

Limited-Slip Collar

The martingale, Greyhound or limited-slip collar is preferred by many dog owners and trainers. It is fixed with an extra loop that tightens when pressure is applied to the leash. The martingale collar gets tighter but does not "choke" the dog. The limited-slip collar should only be used for walking and training, not for free play or interaction with another dog. These types of collar should never be left on the dog, as the extra loop can lead to accidents.

Choke collars, usually made of stainless steel, are made for training purposes but are not recommended for small dogs or heavily coated breeds. The chains can injure small dogs or damage long/abundant coats. Thin nylon choke leads are commonly used on show dogs while in the ring, though they are not practical for everyday use.

The harness, with two or three straps that attach over the dog's shoulders and around his torso, is a humane and safe alternative to the conventional collar. By and large, a well-made harness is virtually escape-proof. Harnesses are available in nylon and mesh and can be outfitted on most dogs, ranging from chest girths of 10 to 30 inches.

Snap-Bolt Choke Collar

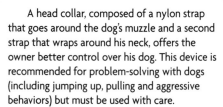

Harness

Nylon Collar

Quick-Click Closure

Snake Chain

Chrome Steel

Fur-Saver

Choke Chain Collars

A head collar, composed of a nylon strap that goes around the dog's muzzle and a second strap that wraps around his neck, offers the owner better control over his dog. This device is recommended for problem-solving with dogs (including jumping up, pulling and aggressive behaviors) but must be used with care.

A training halter, including a flat collar and two straps, made of nylon and webbing, is designed for walking. There are several on the market; some are more difficult to put on the dog than others. The halter harness, with two small slip rings at each end, is recommended for ease of use.

LEASH LIFE

Dogs love leashes! Believe it or not, most dogs dance for joy every time their owners pick up their leashes. The leash means that the dog is going for a walk—and there are few things more exciting than that! Here are some of the kinds of leashes that are commercially available.

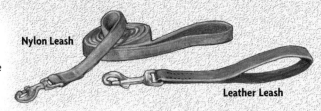

Nylon Leash

Leather Leash

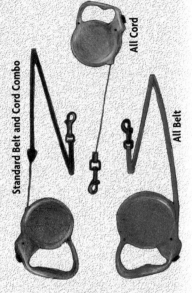

Standard Belt and Cord Combo

All Cord

All Belt

Retractable Leashes

Traditional Leash: Made of cotton, nylon or leather, these leashes are usually about 6 feet in length. A quality-made leather leash is softer on the hands than a nylon one. Durable woven cotton is a popular option. Lengths can vary up to about 48 feet, designed for different uses.

Chain Leash: Usually a metal chain leash with a plastic handle. This is not the best choice for most breeds, as it is heavier than other leashes and difficult to manage.

Retractable Leash: A long nylon cord is housed in a plastic device for extending and retracting. This leash, also known as a flexible leash, is ideal for taking trained dogs for long walks in open areas, although it is not always suitable for large, powerful breeds. Different lengths and sizes are available, so check that you purchase one appropriate for your dog's weight.

Elastic Leash: A nylon leash with an elastic extension. This is useful for well-trained dogs, especially in conjunction with a head halter.

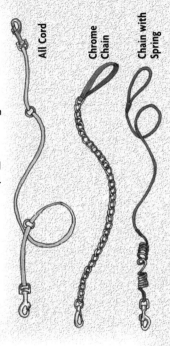

All Cord

Chrome Chain

Chain with Spring

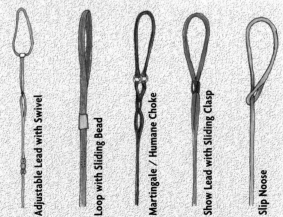

Adjustable Lead with Swivel

Loop with Sliding Bead

Martingale / Humane Choke

Show Lead with Sliding Clasp

Slip Noose

A Variety of Collar-Leash-in-One Products

Avoid leashes that are completely elastic, as they afford minimal control to the handler.

Adjustable Leash: This has two snaps, one on each end, and several metal rings. It is handy if you need to tether your dog temporarily but is never to be used with a choke collar.

Tab Leash: A short leash (4 to 6 inches long) that attaches to your dog's collar. This device serves like a handle, in case you have to grab your dog while he's exercising off lead. It's ideal for "half-trained" dogs or dogs that listen only half of the time.

Slip Leash: Essentially a leash with a collar built in, similar to what a dog-show handler uses to show a dog. This British-style collar has a ring on the end so that you can form a slip collar. Useful if you have to catch your own runaway dog or a stray.

A Dog-Safe Home

The dog-safety police are taking you on a house tour. Let's go room by room and see how safe your own home is for your new pup. The following items are doggy dangers, so either they must be removed or the dog should be monitored or not allowed access to these areas.

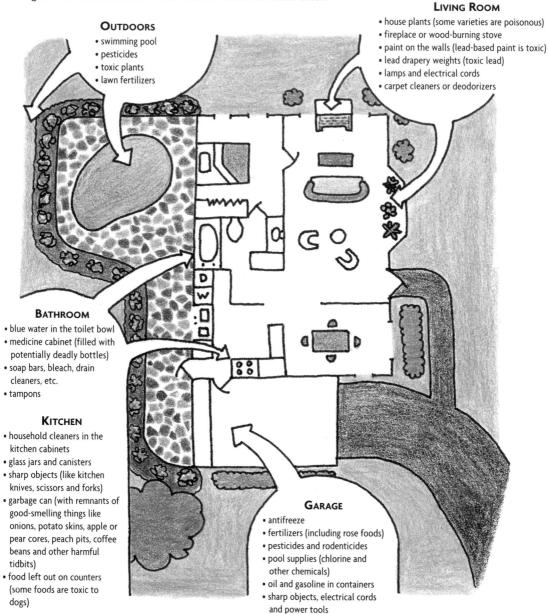

Living Room
- house plants (some varieties are poisonous)
- fireplace or wood-burning stove
- paint on the walls (lead-based paint is toxic)
- lead drapery weights (toxic lead)
- lamps and electrical cords
- carpet cleaners or deodorizers

Outdoors
- swimming pool
- pesticides
- toxic plants
- lawn fertilizers

Bathroom
- blue water in the toilet bowl
- medicine cabinet (filled with potentially deadly bottles)
- soap bars, bleach, drain cleaners, etc.
- tampons

Kitchen
- household cleaners in the kitchen cabinets
- glass jars and canisters
- sharp objects (like kitchen knives, scissors and forks)
- garbage can (with remnants of good-smelling things like onions, potato skins, apple or pear cores, peach pits, coffee beans and other harmful tidbits)
- food left out on counters (some foods are toxic to dogs)

Garage
- antifreeze
- fertilizers (including rose foods)
- pesticides and rodenticides
- pool supplies (chlorine and other chemicals)
- oil and gasoline in containers
- sharp objects, electrical cords and power tools

first, you don't want him wandering too far away from you, and when taking him out for toileting you will want to keep him in the specific area chosen for his potty spot.

Once the puppy is heel trained with a traditional leash, you can consider purchasing a retractable lead. A retractable lead is excellent for walking adult dogs that are already leash-wise. This

> **TOXIC PLANTS**
> Plants are natural puppy magnets, but many can be harmful, even fatal, if ingested by a puppy or adult dog. Scout your yard and home interior and remove any plants, bushes or flowers that could be even mildly dangerous. It could save your puppy's life. You can obtain a complete list of toxic plants from your veterinarian, at the public library or by looking online.

type of lead allows the dog to roam farther away from you and explore a wider area when out walking and also retracts when you need to keep him close to you.

HOME SAFETY FOR YOUR PUPPY

The importance of puppy-proofing cannot be overstated. In addition to making your house comfortable for your Tibetan Terrier's arrival, you also must make sure that your

house is safe for your puppy before you bring him home. There are countless hazards in the owner's personal living environment that a pup can sniff, chew, swallow or destroy. Many

Not every plant is a safe one for your Tibetan Terrier puppy to chew or ingest, and some of the most dangerous plants are fairly common.

Providing safe chew toys will save you money at the shoe store and the vet's office.

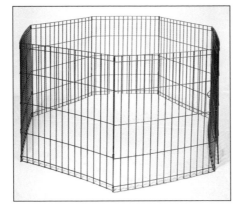

are obvious; others are not. Do a thorough advance house check to remove or rearrange those things that could hurt your puppy, keeping any potentially dangerous items out of areas to which he will have access.

Electrical cords are especially dangerous, since puppies view them as irresistible chew toys. Unplug and remove all exposed cords or fasten them beneath a baseboard where the puppy cannot reach them. Veterinarians and firefighters can tell you horror stories about electrical burns and house fires that resulted from puppy-chewed electrical cords. Consider this a most serious precaution for your puppy and the rest of your family.

Scout your home for tiny objects that might be seen at a pup's eye level. Keep medication bottles and cleaning supplies well out of reach, and do the same with waste baskets and other trash containers. It goes without saying

that you should not use rodent poison or other toxic chemicals in any puppy area and that you must keep such containers safely locked up. You will be amazed at how many places a curious puppy can discover!

Once your house has cleared inspection, check your yard. A sturdy fence, well embedded into the ground, will give your dog a safe place to play and potty. Although Tibetan Terriers are not known to be climbers or fence jumpers, they are still athletic dogs, so a 5- to 6-foot-high fence should be adequate to contain an agile youngster or adult. Check

ARE VACCINATIONS NECESSARY?

Vaccinations are recommended for all puppies by the American Veterinary Medical Association (AVMA). Some vaccines are absolutely necessary, while others depend upon a dog's or puppy's individual exposure to certain diseases or the animal's immune history. Rabies vaccinations are required by law in all 50 states. Some diseases are fatal whereas others are treatable, making the need for vaccinating against the latter questionable. Follow your veterinarian's recommendations to keep your dog fully immunized and protected. You can also review the AVMA directive on vaccinations on their website: www.avma.org.

the fence periodically for necessary repairs. If there is a weak link or space to squeeze through, you can be sure a determined Tibetan Terrier will discover it.

The garage and shed can be hazardous places for a pup, as things like fertilizers, chemicals and tools are usually kept there. It's best to keep these areas off limits to the pup. Antifreeze is especially dangerous to dogs, as they find the taste appealing and it takes only a few licks from the driveway to kill a dog, puppy or adult, small breed or large.

VISITING THE VETERINARIAN

A good veterinarian is your Tibetan Terrier puppy's best health insurance policy. If you do not already have a vet, ask friends and experienced dog people in your area for recommendations so that you can select a vet before you bring your Tibetan Terrier puppy home. Also arrange for your puppy's first veterinary examination beforehand, since many vets have two- and three-week waiting periods and your puppy should visit the vet within a day or so of coming home.

It's important to make sure your puppy's first visit to the vet is a pleasant and positive one. The vet should take great care to befriend the pup and handle him gently to make their first meeting a positive experience. The vet will

PUPPY SHOTS
Puppies are born with natural antibodies that protect them from most canine diseases. They receive more antibodies from the colostrum in their mother's milk. These immunities wear off, however, and must be replaced through a series of vaccines. Puppy shots are given at 3- to 4-week intervals starting at 6 to 8 weeks of age through 12 to 16 weeks of age. Booster shots are given after one year of age, and every one to three years thereafter.

give the pup a thorough physical examination and set up a schedule for vaccinations and other necessary wellness visits. Be sure to show your vet any health and inoculation records, which you should have received from your breeder. Your vet is a great source of canine health informa-

THE FIRST FAMILY MEETING
Your puppy's first day at home should be quiet and uneventful. Despite his wagging tail, he is still wondering where his mom and siblings are! Let him make friends with other members of the family on his own terms; don't overwhelm him. You have a lifetime ahead to get to know each other!

tion, so be sure to ask questions and take notes. Creating a health journal for your puppy will make a handy reference for his wellness and any future health problems that may arise.

MEETING THE FAMILY

Your Tibetan Terrier's homecoming is an exciting time for all members of the family, and it's only natural that everyone will be eager to meet him, pet him and play with him. However, for the puppy's sake, it's best to make these initial family meetings as uneventful as possible so that the pup is not overwhelmed with too much too soon. Remember, he has just left his dam and his littermates and is away from the breeder's home for the first time. Despite his fuzzy wagging tail, he is still apprehensive and

wondering where he is and who all these strange humans are. It's best to let him explore on his own and meet the family members as he feels comfortable. Let him investigate all the new smells, sights and sounds at his own pace. Children should be especially careful to not get overly excited, use loud voices or hug the pup too tightly. Be calm, gentle and affectionate, and be ready to comfort him if he appears frightened or uneasy.

Be sure to show your puppy his new crate during this first day home. Toss a treat or two inside the crate; if he associates the crate with food, he will associate the crate with good things. If he is comfortable with the crate, you can offer him his first meal inside it. Leave the door ajar so he can wander in and out as he chooses.

FIRST NIGHT IN HIS NEW HOME

So much has happened in your Tibetan Terrier puppy's first day away from the breeder. He's had his first car ride to his new home. He's met his new human family and perhaps the other family pets. He has explored his new house and yard, at least those places where he is to be allowed during his first weeks at home. He may have visited his new veterinarian. He has eaten his first meal or two away from his dam and litter-mates. Surely that's enough to tire

If properly introduced and socialized, Tibetan Terriers and young people make ideal friends. Tibetans are playful and protective, making them perfect companions for the whole family.

COST OF OWNERSHIP
The purchase price of your puppy is merely the first expense in the typical dog budget. Quality dog food, veterinary care (sickness and health maintenance), dog supplies and grooming costs will add up to big bucks every year. Can you adequately afford to support a canine addition to the family?

out an eight-week-old Tibetan Terrier pup—or so you hope!

It's bedtime. During the day, the pup investigated his crate, which is his new den and sleeping space, so it is not entirely strange to him. Line the crate with a soft towel or blanket that he can

snuggle into and gently place him into the crate for the night. Some breeders send home a piece of bedding from where the pup slept with his littermates, and those familiar scents are a great comfort for the puppy on his first night without his siblings.

He will probably whine or cry. The puppy is objecting to the confinement and the fact that he is alone for the first time. This can be a stressful time for you as well as for the pup. It's important that you remain strong and don't let the puppy out of his crate to comfort him. He will fall asleep eventually. If you release him, the puppy will learn that crying means "out" and will continue that habit. You are laying the groundwork for future habits. Some breeders find that soft music can soothe a crying pup and help him get to sleep.

SOCIALIZING YOUR PUPPY
The first 20 weeks of your Tibetan Terrier puppy's life are the most important of his entire lifetime. A properly socialized puppy will grow up to be a confident and stable adult who will be a pleasure to live with and a welcome addition to the neighborhood.

The importance of socialization cannot be overemphasized. Research on canine behavior has proven that puppies who are not exposed to new sights, sounds,

THE CRITICAL SOCIALIZATION PERIOD

Canine research has shown that a puppy's 8th through 16th week is the most critical learning period of his life. This is when the puppy "learns to learn," a time when he needs positive experiences to build confidence and stability. Puppies who are not exposed to different people and situations outside the home during this period can grow up to be fearful and sometimes aggressive. This is also the best time for puppy lessons, since he has not yet acquired any bad habits that could undermine his ability to learn.

people and animals during their first 20 weeks of life will grow up to be timid and fearful, even aggressive, and unable to flourish outside of their home environment.

Socializing your puppy is not difficult and, in fact, will be a fun time for you both. Lead training goes hand in hand with socialization, so your puppy will be learning how to walk on a lead at the same time that he's meeting the neighborhood. Because the Tibetan Terrier is such a remarkable breed, everyone will want to meet "the new kid on the block." Take him for short walks, to the park and to other dog-friendly places where he will encounter new people, especially children.

Puppies automatically recognize children as "little people" and are drawn to play with them. Just make sure that you supervise these meetings and that the children do not get too rough or encourage him to play too hard. An overzealous pup can often nip too hard, frightening the child and in turn making the puppy overly excited. A bad experience in puppyhood can impact a dog for life, so a pup that has a negative experience with a child may grow up to be shy or even aggressive around children.

Take your puppy along on your daily errands. Puppies are natural "people magnets," and most people who see your pup will want to pet him. All of these encounters will help to mold him into a confident adult dog. Likewise, you will soon feel like a confident, responsible dog owner,

Like puppies of all other breeds, Tibetan Terrier youngsters must become familiar with the sights, smells and sounds of the world around them if they are to mature properly.

NEW RELEASES

Most breeders release their puppies between seven and ten weeks of age. A breeder who allows puppies to leave the litter at five or six weeks of age may be more concerned with profit than with the puppies' welfare. However, some breeders of show or working breeds may hold one or more top-quality puppies longer, occasionally until three or four months of age, in order to evaluate the puppies' career or show potential and decide which one(s) they will keep for themselves.

rightly proud of your handsome Tibetan Terrier.

Be especially careful of your puppy's encounters and experiences during the eight-to-ten-week-old period, which is also called the "fear period." This is a serious imprinting period, and all contact during this time should be gentle and positive. A frightening or negative event could leave a permanent impression that could affect his future behavior if a similar situation arises.

Also make sure that your puppy has received his first and second rounds of vaccinations before you expose him to other dogs or bring him to places that other dogs may frequent. Avoid dog parks and other strange-dog areas until your vet assures you that your puppy is fully immunized and resistant to the diseases that can be passed between canines. Discuss socialization with your breeder, as some breeders recommend socializing the puppy even before he has received all of his inoculations, depending on how outgoing the puppy may be.

Socialization includes a bit of rough and tumble. Puppies learn from each other the rules of canine society.

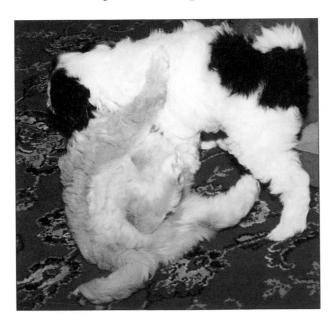

LEADER OF THE PUPPY'S PACK
Like other canines, your puppy needs an authority figure, someone he can look up to and regard as the leader of his "pack." His first pack leader was his dam, who taught him to be polite and not chew too hard on her ears or nip at her muzzle. He learned those same lessons from his litter-

mates. If he played too rough, they cried in pain and stopped the game, which sent an important message to the rowdy puppy.

As puppies play together, they are also struggling to determine who will be the boss. Being pack animals, dogs need someone to be in charge. If a litter of puppies remained together beyond puppyhood, one of the pups would emerge as the strongest one, the one who calls the shots.

Once your puppy leaves the pack, he will look intuitively for a new leader. If he does not recognize you as that leader, he will try to assume that position for himself. Of course, it is hard to imagine your adorable Tibetan Terrier puppy trying to be in charge when he is so small and seemingly helpless. You must remember that these are natural canine instincts. Do not cave in and allow your pup to get the upper "paw"!

Just as socialization is so important during these first 20 weeks, so too is your puppy's early education. He was born without any bad habits. He does not know what is good or bad behavior. If he does things like nipping and digging, it's because he is having fun and doesn't know that humans consider these things as "bad." It's your job to teach him proper puppy manners, and this is the best time to accomplish that—before he has developed bad

Your Tibetan Terrier puppy quite literally looks up to you as his pack leader.

habits, since it is much more difficult to "unlearn" or correct unacceptable learned behavior than to teach good behavior from the start.

Make sure that all members of the family understand the importance of being consistent when training their new puppy. If you tell the puppy to stay off the sofa and your daughter allows him to cuddle on the couch to watch her favorite television show, your pup will be confused about what he is and is not allowed to do. Have a family conference before your pup comes home so that everyone understands the basic principles of puppy training and the rules you have set forth for the pup, and agrees to follow them.

The old saying that "an ounce of prevention is worth a pound of

WATCH THE WATER
To help your puppy sleep through the night without having to relieve himself, remove his water bowl after 7 p.m. Offer him a couple of ice cubes during the evening to quench his thirst. Never leave water in a puppy's crate, as this is inviting puddles of mishaps.

cure" is especially true when it comes to puppies. It is much easier to prevent inappropriate behavior than it is to change it. It's also easier and less stressful for the pup, since it will keep discipline to a minimum and create a more positive learning environment for him. That, in turn, will also be easier on you.

Here are a few commonsense tips to keep your belongings safe and your puppy out of trouble:

- Keep your closet doors closed and your shoes, socks and other apparel off the floor so your puppy can't get to them.
- Keep a secure lid on the trash container or put the trash where your puppy can't dig into it. He can't damage what he can't reach!
- Supervise your puppy at all times to make sure he is not getting into mischief. If he starts to chew the corner of the rug, you can distract him instantly by tossing a toy for him to fetch. You also will be able to whisk him outside when you notice that he is about to piddle on the carpet. If you can't see your puppy, you can't teach or correct his behavior.

SOLVING PUPPY PROBLEMS

CHEWING AND NIPPING
Nipping at fingers and toes is normal puppy behavior. Chewing is also the way that puppies investigate their surroundings. However, you will have to teach your puppy that chewing anything other than his toys is not acceptable. That won't happen overnight and at times puppy teeth will test your patience. However, if you allow nipping and chewing to continue, just think about the damage that a mature Tibetan Terrier can do with a full set of adult teeth.

TASTY LESSONS

The best route to teaching a very young puppy is through his tummy. Use tiny bits of soft puppy treats to teach obedience commands like come, sit and down. Don't overdo treats: schooltime is not meant to be mealtime.

Whenever your puppy nips your hand or fingers, cry out "Ouch!" in a loud voice, which should startle your puppy and stop him from nipping, even if only for a moment. Immediately distract him by offering a small treat or an appropriate toy for him to chew instead (which means having chew toys and puppy treats handy or in your pockets at all times). Praise him when he takes the toy and tell him what a good fellow he is. Praise is just as or even more important in puppy training as discipline and correction.

Puppies also tend to nip at children more often than adults, since they perceive little ones to be more vulnerable and more similar to their littermates. Teach your children appropriate responses to nipping behavior. If they are unable to handle it themselves, you may have to intervene. Puppy nips can be quite painful and a child's frightened reaction will only encourage a puppy to nip harder, which is a natural canine response. As with all other puppy situations, interaction between your Tibetan Terrier puppy and children should be supervised.

Chewing on objects, not just family members' fingers and ankles, is also normal canine behavior that can be especially tedious (for the owner, not the pup) during the teething period when the puppy's adult teeth are coming in. At this stage, chewing just plain feels good. Furniture legs and cabinet corners are common puppy favorites. Shoes and other personal items also taste pretty good to a pup.

The best solution is, once again, prevention. If you value something, keep it tucked away and out of reach. You can't hide your dining-room table in a closet, but you can try to deflect the chewing by applying a bitter product made just to deter dogs from chewing. Available in a spray or cream, this substance is vile-tasting, although safe for

Puppies will welcome almost anything for play; be careful that the chosen playthings are safe for the curious and active Tibetan.

BE CONSISTENT

Consistency is a key element, in fact is absolutely necessary, to a puppy's learning environment. A behavior (such as chewing, jumping up or climbing onto the furniture) cannot be forbidden one day and then allowed the next. That will only confuse the pup, and he will not understand what he is supposed to do. Just one or two episodes of allowing an undesirable behavior to "slide" will imprint that behavior on a puppy's brain and make that behavior more difficult to erase or change.

dogs, and most puppies will avoid the forbidden object after one tiny taste. You also can apply the product to your leather leash if the puppy tries to chew on his lead during leash-training sessions.

Keep a ready supply of safe chews handy to offer your Tibetan Terrier as a distraction when he starts to chew on something that's a "no-no." Remember, at this tender age he does not yet know what is permitted or forbidden, so you have to be "on call" every minute he's awake and on the prowl.

You may lose a treasure or two during puppy's growing-up period, and the furniture could sustain a nasty nick or two. These can be trying times, so be prepared for those inevitable accidents and comfort yourself in knowing that this too shall pass.

PUPPY WHINING

Puppies often cry and whine, just as infants and little children do. It's their way of telling us that they are lonely or in need of attention. Your puppy will miss his littermates and will feel insecure when he is left alone. You may be out of the house or just in another room, but he will still feel alone. During these times, the puppy's crate should be his personal comfort station, a place all his own where he can feel safe and secure. Once he learns that being alone is okay and not something to be feared, he will settle down without crying or objecting. You might want to leave a radio on while he is crated, as the sound of human voices can be soothing and will give the impression that people are around.

Give your puppy a favorite cuddly toy or chew toy to entertain him whenever he is crated. You will both be happier: the puppy because he is safe in his den and you because he is quiet, safe and not getting into puppy escapades that can wreak havoc in your house or cause him danger.

To make sure that your puppy will always view his crate as a safe and cozy place, never,

Puppies that have been acclimated to the dog crate at the breeder's kennel will adjust better to crate training once they arrive in their new homes.

ever use the crate as punishment. That's the best way to turn the crate into a negative place that the pup will want to avoid. Sure, you can use the crate for your own peace of mind if your puppy is getting into trouble and needs some "time out." Just don't let him know that! Never scold the pup and immediately place him into the crate. Count to ten, give him a couple of hugs and maybe a treat, then scoot him into his crate.

It's also important not to make a big fuss when he is released from the crate. That will make getting out of the crate more appealing than being in the crate, which is just the opposite of what you are trying to achieve.

TIBETAN TERRIER

Adding a Tibetan Terrier to your household means adding a new family member who will need your care each and every day. When your Tibetan Terrier pup first comes home, you will start a routine with him so that, as he grows up, your dog will have a daily schedule just as you do. The aspects of your dog's daily care will likewise become regular parts of your day, so you'll both have a new schedule. Dogs learn by consistency and thrive on routine: regular times for meals, exercise, grooming and potty trips are just as important for your dog as they are to you! Your dog's schedule will depend much on your family's daily routine, but remember that you now have a new member of the family who is part of your day every day.

FEEDING

Feeding your dog the best diet is based on various factors, including age, activity level, overall condition and size of breed. When you visit the breeder, he will share with you his advice about the proper diet for your dog based on his experience with the breed and the foods with which he has had success. Likewise, your vet will be a helpful source of advice throughout the dog's life and will aid you in planning a diet for optimal health.

FEEDING THE PUPPY

Of course, your pup's very first food will be his dam's milk. There may be special situations in which pups fail to nurse, necessitating that the breeder hand-feed them with a formula, but for the most part pups spend the first weeks of life nursing from their dam. The breeder weans the pups by gradually introducing solid foods and

Fresh water is a very important component of a healthy diet. You may, however, have to convince your puppy of this.

decreasing the milk meals. Pups may even start themselves off on the weaning process, albeit inadvertently, if they snatch bites from their mom's food bowl.

By the time the pups are ready for new homes, they are fully weaned and eating a good puppy food. As a new owner, you may be thinking, "Great! The breeder has taken care of the hard part." Not so fast.

DIET DON'TS

- Got milk? Don't give it to your dog! Dogs cannot tolerate large quantities of cows' milk, as they do not have the enzymes to digest lactose.
- You may have heard of dog owners who add raw eggs to their dogs' food for a shiny coat or to make the food more palatable, but consumption of raw eggs too often can cause a deficiency of the vitamin biotin.
- Avoid feeding table scraps, as they will upset the balance of the dog's complete food. Additionally, fatty or highly seasoned foods can cause upset canine stomachs.
- Do not offer raw meat to your dog. Raw meat can contain parasites; it also is high in fat.
- Vitamin A toxicity in dogs can be caused by too much raw liver, especially if the dog already gets enough vitamin A in his balanced diet, which should be the case.
- Bones like chicken, pork chop and other soft bones are not suitable, as they easily splinter.

A puppy's first year of life is the time when all or most of his growth and development takes place. This is a delicate time, and diet plays a huge role in proper skeletal and muscular formation. Improper diet and exercise habits can lead to damaging problems that will compromise the dog's health and movement for his entire life. That being said, new owners should not worry needlessly. With the myriad types of food formulated specifically for growing pups of different-sized breeds, dog-food manufacturers have taken much of the guesswork out of feeding your puppy well. Since growth-food formulas are designed to provide the nutrition that a growing puppy needs, it is unnecessary and, in fact, can prove harmful to add supplements to the diet. Research has shown that too much of certain vitamin supplements and

Tibetan Terrier dams are instinctive moms, protective and sensible. The puppies learn manners and their first lessons from their dam.

Your pup's breeder will have introduced him and his littermates to solid food well before you take him home—and a very pleasant introduction it must have been!

same times and in the same place each day is important for both housebreaking purposes and establishing the dog's everyday routine. As for the amount to feed, growing puppies generally need proportionately more food per body weight than their adult counterparts, but a pup should never be allowed to gain excess weight. Dogs of all ages should be kept in proper body condition, but extra weight can strain a pup's developing frame, causing skeletal problems.

minerals predispose a dog to skeletal problems. It's by no means a case of "if a little is good, a lot is better." At every stage of your dog's life, too much or too little in the way of nutrients can be harmful, which is why a manufactured complete food is the easiest way to know that your dog is getting what he needs.

Because of a young pup's small body and accordingly small digestive system, his daily portion will be divided up into small meals throughout the day. This can mean starting off with three or more meals a day and decreasing the number of meals as the pup matures. Eventually you can feed only one meal a day, although it is generally thought that dividing the day's food into two meals on a morning/evening schedule is healthier for the dog's digestion.

Regarding the feeding schedule, feeding the pup at the

Watch your pup's weight as he grows and, if the recommended amounts seem to be too much or too little for your pup, consult the vet about appropriate dietary changes. Keep in mind that treats, although small, can quickly add up throughout the day, contributing unnecessary calories. Treats are fine when used prudently; opt for dog treats specially formulated to be healthy or for nutritious snacks like small pieces of cheese or cooked chicken.

FEEDING THE ADULT DOG

For the adult (meaning physically mature) dog, feeding properly is about maintenance, not growth. Again, correct weight is a concern. Your dog should appear fit and should have an evident "waist." His ribs should not be protruding (a sign of being underweight), but they should be covered by only a slight layer of fat. Under normal circumstances, an adult dog can be maintained fairly easily with a high-quality nutritionally complete adult-formula food.

Factor treats into your dog's overall daily caloric intake, and avoid offering table scraps. Overweight dogs are more prone to health problems. Research has even shown that obesity takes years off a dog's life. With that in mind, resist the urge to overfeed and over-treat. Don't make unnecessary additions to your dog's diet, whether with tidbits or with extra vitamins and minerals.

The amount of food needed for proper maintenance will vary depending on the individual dog's activity level, but you will be able to tell whether the daily portions are keeping him in good shape. With the wide variety of good complete foods available, choosing what to feed is largely a matter of personal preference. Just as with the puppy, the adult dog should have consistency in his mealtimes and feeding place. In addition to a consistent routine, regular mealtimes also allow the owner to see how much his dog is eating. If the dog seems never to be satisfied or, likewise, becomes uninterested in his food, the owner will know right away that something is wrong and can consult the vet.

DIETS FOR THE AGING DOG

A good rule of thumb is that once a dog has reached 75% of his expected lifespan, he has reached "senior citizen" or geriatric status. Your Tibetan Terrier will be considered a senior at about nine years of age; based on his size, he has a projected lifespan of about 13 years. (The smallest breeds generally enjoy the longest lives and the largest breeds the shortest.)

SWITCHING FOODS

There are certain times in a dog's life when it becomes necessary to switch his food; for example, from puppy to adult food and then from adult to senior-dog food. Additionally, you may decide to feed your pup a different type of food from what he received from the breeder, and there may be "emergency" situations in which you can't find your dog's normal brand and have to offer something else temporarily. Anytime a change is made, for whatever reason, the switch must be done gradually. You don't want to upset the dog's stomach or end up with a picky eater who refuses to eat something new. A tried-and-true approach is, over the course of about a week, to mix a little of the new food in with the old, increasing the proportion of new to old as the days progress. At the end of the week, you'll be feeding his regular portions of the new food, and he will barely notice the change.

What does aging have to do with your dog's diet? No, he won't get a discount at the local diner's early-bird special. Yes, he will require some dietary changes to accommodate the changes that come along with increased age. One change is that the older dog's dietary needs become more similar to that of a puppy. Specifically, dogs can metabolize more protein as youngsters and seniors than in the adult-maintenance stage. Discuss with your vet whether you need to switch to a higher-protein or senior-formulated food or whether your current adult-dog food contains sufficient nutrition for the senior.

Watching the dog's weight remains essential, even more so in the senior stage. Older dogs are already more vulnerable to illness, and obesity only contributes to their susceptibility to problems. As the older dog becomes less

This tidy Tibetan wears a snood to keep his ear furnishings clean during mealtime.

WEIGHT AND SEE!

When you look at yourself in the mirror each day, you get very used to what you see! It's only when you pull out last year's vacation outfit and can't zipper it that you notice that you've put on some pounds. Dog owners are the same way with their dogs. Often a few pounds go unnoticed, and it's not until some time passes or the vet remarks that your dog looks more than pleasantly plump that you realize what's happened. To avoid your pet's becoming obese right under your very nose, make a habit of routinely evaluating his condition with a hands-on test.

Can you feel, but not see, your dog's rib cage? Does your dog have a waist? His waist should be evident by touch and also visible from above and from the side. In top view, the dog's body should have an hourglass shape. These are indicators of good condition.

While it's not hard to spot a skinny or overly rotund dog, it's the subtle changes that lead up to under- or overweight condition of which we must be aware. If your dog's ribs are visible, he is too thin. Conversely, if you can't feel the ribs under too much fat, and if there's no indication of a waistline, your dog is overweight. Both of these conditions require changes to the diet. A trip or sometimes just a call to the vet will help you modify your dog's feeding.

active and thus exercises less, his regular portions may cause him to gain weight. At this point, you may consider decreasing his daily food intake or switching to a reduced-calorie food. As with other changes, you should consult your vet for advice.

TYPES OF FOOD AND READING THE LABEL

When selecting the type of food to feed your dog, it is important to check out the label for ingredients. Many dry-food products have soybean, corn or rice as the main ingredient. The main ingredient will be listed first on the label, with the rest of the ingredients following in descending order according to their proportion in the food. While these types of dry food are fine, you should also look into dry foods based on meat or fish. These are better-quality foods and thus higher priced. However, they may be just as economical in the long run because studies have shown that it takes less of the higher-quality foods to maintain a dog.

Comparing the various types of food, dry, canned and semi-moist, dry foods contain the least amount of water and canned foods the most. Proportionately, dry foods are the most calorie- and nutrient-dense, which means that you need more of a canned food product to supply the same amount of nutrition. In

households domiciling breeds of disparate size, the canned/dry/semi-moist question can be of special importance. Larger breeds obviously eat more than smaller ones and thus in general do better on dry foods, but smaller breeds do fine on canned foods and require "small bite" formulations to protect their small mouths and teeth if fed only dry foods. So if you have breeds of different size in your household, consider both your own preferences and what your dogs like to eat, but in the main think canned for the little guys and dry or semi-moist for everyone else. You may find success mixing the food types as well. Water is important for all

VARIETY IS THE SPICE

Although dog-food manufacturers contend that dogs don't like variety in their diets, studies show quite the opposite to be true. Dogs would much rather vary their meals than eat the same old chow day in and day out. Dry kibble is no more exciting for a dog than the same bowl of bran flakes would be for you. Fortunately, there are dozens of varieties available on the market, and your dog will likely show preference for certain flavors over others. A word of warning: don't overdo it or you'll develop a fussy eater who only prefers chopped beef fillet and asparagus tips every night.

As any experienced breeder will tell you, first you breed a coat and then you feed a coat. The diet of your Tibetan will affect his coat throughout the course of his life.

dogs, but even more so for those fed dry foods, as there is no high water content in their food.

There are strict controls that regulate the nutritional content of dog food, and a food has to meet the minimum requirements in order to be considered "complete and balanced." It is important that you choose such a food for your

dog, so check the label to be sure that your chosen food meets the requirements. If not, look for a food that clearly states on the label that it is formulated to be complete and balanced for your dog's particular stage of life.

Recommendations for amounts to feed will also be indicated on the label. You should also ask your vet about proper food portions, and you will keep an eye on your dog's condition to see whether the recommended amounts are adequate. If he becomes over- or underweight, you will need to make adjustments; this also would be a good time to consult your vet.

The food label may also make feeding suggestions, such as whether moistening a dry-food product is recommended. Sometimes a splash of water will make the food more palatable for the dog and even enhance the flavor. Don't be overwhelmed by the many factors that go into feeding your dog. Manufacturers of complete and balanced foods make it easy, and once you find the right food and amounts for your Tibetan Terrier, his daily feeding will be a matter of routine.

DON'T FORGET THE WATER!

For a dog, it's always time for a drink! Regardless of what type of food he eats, there's no doubt that he needs plenty of water. Fresh cold water, in a clean bowl, should be freely available to your dog at all times. There are special circumstances, such as during puppy housebreaking, when you will want to monitor your pup's water intake so that you will be able to predict when he will need to relieve himself, but water must be available to him nonetheless.

Water is essential for hydration and proper body function just as it is in humans.

You will get to know how much your dog typically drinks in a day. Of course, in the heat or if exercising vigorously, he will be more thirsty and will drink more. However, if he begins to drink noticeably more water for no apparent reason, this could signal any of various problems, and you are advised to consult your vet.

Water is the best drink for dogs. Some owners are tempted to give milk from time to time or to moisten dry food with milk, but dogs do not have the enzymes

QUENCHING HIS THIRST

Is your dog drinking more than normal and trying to lap up everything in sight? Excessive drinking has many different causes. Obvious causes for a dog's being thirstier than usual are hot weather and vigorous exercise. However, if your dog is drinking more for no apparent reason, you could have cause for concern. Serious conditions like kidney or liver disease, diabetes and various types of hormonal problems can all be indicated by excessive drinking. If you notice your dog's being excessively thirsty, contact your vet at once. Hopefully there will be a simpler explanation, but the earlier a serious problem is detected, the sooner it can be treated, with a better rate of cure.

necessary to digest the lactose in milk, which is much different from the milk that nursing puppies receive. Therefore, stick with clean fresh water to quench your dog's thirst, and always have it readily available to him.

Don't let the TT's cuteness and glamour fool you—this is an active dog who likes to be out and about, enjoying fun sports with his family and friends.

EXERCISE

Although Tibetan Terriers seem ready to accept as much or as little exercise as their owners will give them, this is an active breed, so it is only fair to give them an opportunity for a good amount of exercise, both by way of free running and walking on a lead. When a Tibetan Terrier is kept with another dog, the two will also find opportunities to create their own exercise through play.

Muscles need to be kept in good, firm condition, and exercise, even lead walking, stimulates not only the muscles but also the mind. Always remember, though, that Tibetan Terriers are capable of running fast, so they should only be let off lead in areas where you are entirely certain they can come to no harm.

Keep in mind that a Tibetan Terrier running free, while thoroughly enjoying the outing, stands every chance of getting both wet and dirty, as well as picking up lots of debris in the long coat. Long-term exposure to dampness can result in aching limbs, especially for the older dog, so you will need to get the coat back into tip-top condition upon your return, also removing anything picked up in the coat so that knots do not form.

Tibetan Terriers are good jumpers, and those kept in a kennel situation, or an environment where they do not have access to free exercise areas, appreciate different levels on which to jump and to sit, though these should never be so high that they might cause injury.

SELECTING THE RIGHT BRUSHES AND COMBS

Will a rubber curry make my dog look slicker? Is a rake smaller than a pin brush? Do I choose nylon or natural bristles? Buying a dog brush can make the hairs on your head stand on end! Here's a quick once-over to educate you on the different types of brushes.

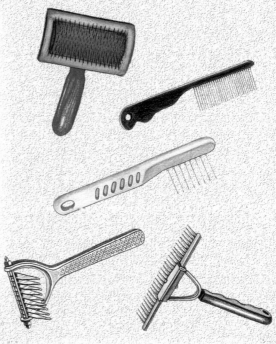

Slicker Brush: Fine metal prongs closely set on a curved base. Used to remove dead coat from the undercoat of medium- to long-coated breeds.

Pin Brush: Metal pins, often covered with rubber tips, set on an oval base. Used to remove shedding hair and is gentler than a slicker brush.

Metal Comb: Steel teeth attached to a steel handle; the closeness and size of the teeth vary greatly. A "flea comb" has tiny teeth set very closely together and is used to find fleas in a dog's coat. Combs with wider teeth are used for detangling longer coats.

Rake: Long-toothed comb with a short handle. Used to remove undercoat from heavily coated breeds with dense undercoats.

Soft-bristle Brush: Nylon or natural bristles set in a plastic or wood base. Used on short coats or long coats (without undercoats).

Rubber Curry: Rubber prongs, with or without a handle. Used for short-coated dogs. Good for use during shampooing.

Combination Brushes: Two-sided brush with a different type of bristle on each side; for example, pin brush on one side and slicker on the other, or bristle brush on one side and pin brush on the other. An economical choice if you need two kinds of brushes.

Grooming Glove: Sometimes called a hound glove; used to give sleek-coated dogs a once-over.

The Tibetan Terrier should become accustomed to daily brushing at an early age.

The "armpits" require special attention. The coat is easily matted here, yet they are sensitive areas and need a gentle touch.

GROOMING

Your Tibetan Terrier will need to be groomed regularly, so it is essential that short grooming sessions be introduced from an early age. From the very beginning a few minutes each day should be set aside, the duration building up slowly as the puppy matures and the coat grows in length. Your puppy should be taught to stand on a solid surface for grooming, a suitable table on which the dog will not slip, but under no circumstances leave your dog alone on a table for fear of injury.

To begin with, just introduce a few gentle brush strokes. Be sure you don't tug at any knots at this stage, for this would cause him to associate grooming sessions with discomfort.

You will notice that your

Tibetan Terrier's coat not only grows longer with age but eventually changes from a puppy coat to an adult one. This will be a difficult time when knots will form all too easily, and you will realize how comparatively easy grooming your youngster has been until then!

You will certainly need to groom the coat between bath times, but never groom the coat when it is completely dry. To avoid breaking the ends, use a light conditioning spray; even water dispensed from a fine-spray bottle is better than no moisture at all.

ROUTINE GROOMING

The coat should be parted, layered and brushed section by section, always in the direction of the coat growth. It is imperative to groom right down to the skin so that the undercoat is not left matted. After using a good-quality bristle brush, a wide-toothed comb can be used to finish each section.

If you do find mats in your Tibetan Terrier's coat, spray the mat with a generous amount of conditioning or anti-tangle spray. Leave this to soak in for a few moments, then gently tease out the mat with your fingers. Always work from the inside out, or the knot will just get tighter! Tight knots will probably need to be teased out using a wide-toothed comb, but don't tug at the knot for this will be painful and will also take out too much coat.

Take care grooming the tummy and under the armpits, for these areas are especially sensitive. Whatever you do, take care not to cut through a nipple— and remember that males have little nipples too!

To prevent knots and tangles, be sure to immediately remove any debris which may have accumulated following a visit outdoors. Also, always check your dog's back end to see that nothing remains attached to the coat from his toilet. Between baths you may like to use a damp

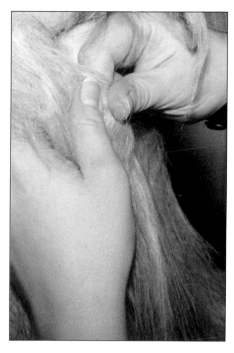

Mats are gently removed with the fingers, working from the inside out.

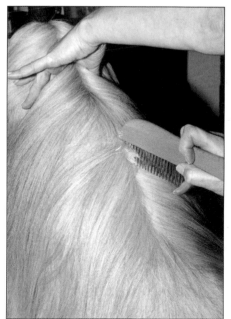

The hair is parted and brushed in sections.

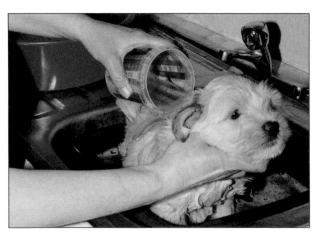

Pups don't require a large bath enclosure, but they should be provided with a non-slip surface on which to stand.

practice to take a wide-toothed comb to create a straight parting down the length of the back so that the coat falls evenly on either side. However, this was not always the case, and there are still a few who prefer not to part the hair.

"Pet Trim"

Although the vast majority of Tibetan Terriers are kept in long coat, a few owners choose to keep their Tibetans in pet trim. The coat is cut down to a more manageable length, usually at a grooming parlor. Tibetan Terriers in pet trim still look very attractive, and this is far better than keeping a pet with a long, uncomfortably matted coat, simply because regular grooming has been neglected. Having said that, even a Tibetan Terrier in shorter coat still needs frequent grooming!

sponge, but always be sure to dry the coat thoroughly.

Some dogs don't seem to mind having their feet groomed; others hate it. Nonetheless, you will have to check feet thoroughly on a regular basis. Be sure you don't allow knots to build up between the toes, and always keep an eye on the length of the toenails.

The Head and the Finishing Touches

It is essential to keep head furnishings and eyes clean, so these must be checked every day. Some owners find it useful to put a specially made "snood" over the head and ears while the dog is eating to prevent soiling.

When grooming your Tibetan Terrier, pay special attention to the hair behind the ear, for this can be of a finer texture and knots easily. When grooming is complete, it is now normal

Bathing

In general, dogs need to be bathed only a few times a year, possibly more often if your dog gets into something messy or if he starts to smell like a dog. Show dogs are usually bathed before every show, which could be as frequent as weekly, although this depends on the owner. Bathing too frequently can have negative effects on the skin and coat, removing natural oils and causing dryness.

If you give your dog his first

bath when he is young, he will become accustomed to the process. Wrestling a dog into the tub or chasing a freshly shampooed dog who has escaped from the bath will be no fun! Most dogs don't naturally enjoy their baths, but you at least want yours to cooperate with you.

Before bathing the dog, have the items you'll need close at hand. First, decide where you will bathe the dog. You should have a tub or basin with a non-slip surface. Puppies can even be bathed in a sink. In warm weather, some like to use a portable pool in the yard, although you'll want to make sure your dog doesn't head for the nearest dirt pile following his bath! You will also need a hose or shower spray to wet the coat thoroughly, a shampoo formulated for dogs, absorbent towels and perhaps a blow dryer. Human shampoos are too harsh for dogs' coats and will dry them out.

Before wetting the dog, give him a brush-through to remove any dead hair, dirt and mats. Make sure he is at ease in the tub and have the water at a comfortable temperature. Begin bathing by wetting the coat all the way down to the skin. Massage in the shampoo, keeping it away from his face and eyes. Rinse him thoroughly, again avoiding the eyes and ears, as you don't want to get water into the ear canals. A

Only use shampoo made specifically for dogs, working the lather all the way to the skin.

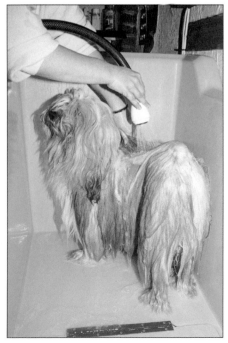

After washing the coat, rinse the coat thoroughly, leaving no traces of shampoo.

Whether dried with a towel or a blow dryer, your pup should not be exposed to drafts.

thorough rinsing is important, as shampoo residue is drying and itchy to the dog. After rinsing, wrap him in a towel to absorb the initial moisture. You can finish drying with either a towel or a blow dryer on low heat, held at a safe distance from the dog. You should keep the dog indoors and away from drafts until he is completely dry.

Clipping your pup's nails while he's young and easy to control will make him amenable to clipping later in life.

NAIL CLIPPING

Having their nails trimmed is not on many dogs' lists of favorite things to do. With this in mind, you will need to accustom your puppy to the procedure at a young age so that he will sit still (well, as still as he can) for his pedicures. Long nails can cause the dog's feet to spread, which is not good for him; likewise, long nails can hurt if they unintentionally scratch, not good for you!

Some dogs' nails are worn down naturally by regular walking on hard surfaces, so the frequency with which you clip depends on your individual dog. Look at his nails from time to time and clip as needed; a good way to know when it's time for a trim is if you hear your dog clicking as he walks across the floor.

There are several types of nail clippers and even electric nail-grinding tools made for dogs. First we'll discuss using the clipper. To start, have your clipper ready and some doggie treats on hand. You want your pup to view his nail-clipping sessions in a positive light, and what better way to convince him than with food?

You may want to enlist the help of an assistant to comfort the pup and offer treats as you concentrate on the clipping itself. The guillotine-type clipper is thought of by many as the easiest type to use; the nail tip is inserted into the opening, and blades on the top and bottom snip it off in one clip.

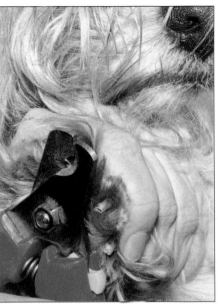

Close-up of the guillotine-type clipper in operation.

THE MONTHLY GRIND

If your dog doesn't like the feeling of nail clippers or if you're not comfortable using them, you may wish to try an electric nail grinder. This tool has a small sandpaper disc on the end that rotates to grind the nails down. Some feel that using a grinder reduces the risk of cutting into the quick; this can be true if the tool is used properly. Usually you will be able to tell where the quick is before you get to it. A benefit of the grinder is that it creates a smooth finish on the nails so that there are no ragged edges.

Because the tool makes noise, your dog should be introduced to it before the actual grinding takes place. Turn it on and let your dog hear the noise; turn it off and let him inspect it with you holding it. Use the grinder gently, holding it firmly and progressing a little at a time until you reach the proper length. Look at the nail as you grind so that you do not go too short. Stop at any indication that you are nearing the quick. It will take a few sessions for both you and the puppy to get used to the grinder. Make sure that you don't let his hair get tangled in the grinder!

Start by grasping the pup's paw; a little pressure on the foot pad causes the nail to extend, making it easier to clip. Clip off a little at a time. If you can see the "quick," which is a blood vessel that runs through each nail, you will know how much to trim, as you do not want to cut into the quick. On that note, if you do cut the quick, which will cause bleeding, you can stem the flow of blood with a styptic pencil or other clotting agent. If you mistakenly nip the quick, do not panic or fuss, as this will cause the pup to be afraid. Simply reassure the pup, stop the bleeding and move on to the next nail. Don't be discouraged; you will become a professional canine pedicurist with practice.

Plucking the hairs from the ears is a simple task once you learn how to do it.

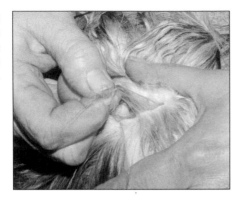

The ears should be gently cleaned with cotton wipes available from your local pet shop.

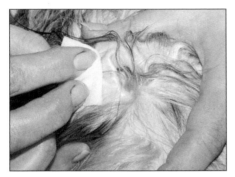

You may or may not be able to see the quick, so it's best to just clip off a small bit at a time. If you see a dark dot in the center of the nail, this is the quick and your cue to stop clipping. Tell the puppy he's a "good boy" and offer a piece of treat with each nail. You can also use nail-clipping time to examine the footpads, making sure that they are not dry and cracked and that nothing has become embedded in them.

The nail grinder, the other choice, is many owners' first choice. Accustoming the puppy to the sound of the grinder and sensation of the buzz presents

fewer challenges than the clipper, and there's no chance of cutting through the quick. Use the grinder on a low setting and always talk soothingly to your dog. He won't mind his salon visit, and he'll have nicely polished nails as well.

EAR CLEANING
While keeping your dog's ears clean unfortunately will not cause him to "hear" your commands any better, it will protect him from ear infection and ear-mite infestation. In addition, a dog's ears are vulnerable to waxy build-up and to collecting foreign matter from the outdoors. Look in your dog's ears regularly to ensure that they look pink, clean and otherwise healthy. Even if they look fine, an odor in the ears signals a problem and means it's time to call the vet.

A dog's ears should be cleaned regularly; once a week is suggested, and you can do this along with your regular brushing. Using a cotton ball or pad and never probing into the ear canal, wipe the ear gently. You can use an ear-cleansing liquid or powder available from your vet or pet-supply store; alternatively, you might prefer to use homemade solutions with ingredients like one part white vinegar and one part hydrogen peroxide. Ask your vet about home remedies before you attempt to concoct something on your own!

THE EARS KNOW

Examining your puppy's ears helps ensure good internal health. The ears are the eyes to the dog's innards! Begin handling your puppy's ears when he's still young so that he doesn't protest every time you lift a flap or touch his ears. Yeast and bacteria are two of the culprits that you can detect by examining the ear. You will notice a strong, often foul, odor, debris, redness or some kind of discharge. All of these point to health problems that can worsen over time. Additionally, you are on the lookout for wax accumulation, ear mites and other tiny bothersome parasites and their even tinier droppings. You may have to pluck hair with tweezers in order to have a better view into the dog's ears, but this is painless if done carefully.

Keep your dog's ears free of excess hair by plucking it as needed. If done gently, this will be painless for the dog. Look for wax, brown droppings (a sign of ear mites), redness or any other abnormalities. At the first sign of a problem, contact your vet so that he can prescribe an appropriate medication.

EYE CARE

During grooming sessions, pay extra attention to the condition of your dog's eyes. If the area around the eyes is soiled or if tear staining has occurred, there are various cleaning agents made especially for this purpose. Look at the dog's eyes to make sure no debris has entered; dogs with large eyes and those who spend time outdoors are especially prone to this.

The signs of an eye infection are obvious: mucus, redness, puffiness, scabs or other signs of irritation. If your dog's eyes become infected, the vet will likely prescribe an antibiotic ointment for treatment. If you notice signs of more serious problems, such as opacities in the eye, which usually indicate cataracts, consult the vet at once. Taking time to pay attention to your dog's eyes will alert you in

Indoors or outdoors, the well-groomed Tibetan Terrier makes a pretty picture.

PRESERVING THOSE PEARLY WHITES

What do you treasure more than the smile of your beloved canine pal? Brushing your dog's teeth is just as important as brushing your own. Neglecting your dog's teeth can lead to tooth loss, periodontal disease and inflamed gums, not to mention bad breath. Can you find the time to brush your dog's teeth every day? If not, you should do so once a week at the very least, though every day is truly the ideal. Your vet should give your dog a thorough dental examination during his annual check-ups.

Pet shops sell terrific tooth-care devices, including specially designed toothbrushes, yummy toothpastes and finger-model brushes. You can use a human toothbrush with soft bristles, but never use human toothpastes, which can damage the dog's enamel. Baking soda is an alternative to doggie toothpastes, but your dog will be more receptive to canine toothpastes with the flavor of liver or hamburger. Make tooth care fun for your dog. Let him think that you're "horsing around" with his mouth. When brushing the dog's teeth, begin with the largest teeth (the canines) and proceed back toward the molars.

A CLEAN SMILE

Another essential part of grooming is brushing your dog's teeth and checking his overall oral condition. Studies show that around 80% of dogs experience dental problems by two years of age, and the percentage is higher in older dogs. Therefore it is highly likely that your dog will have trouble with his teeth and gums unless you are proactive with home dental care.

The most common dental problem in dogs is plaque build-up. If not treated, this causes gum disease, infection and resultant tooth loss. Bacteria from these infections spread throughout the body, affecting the vital organs. Do you need much more convincing to start brushing your dog's teeth? If so, take a good whiff of your dog's breath, and read on.

Fortunately, home dental care is rather easy and convenient for pet owners. Specially formulated canine toothpaste is easy to find. You should use one of these toothpastes, not a product for humans. Some doggie pastes are even available in flavors appealing to dogs. If your dog likes the flavor, he will tolerate the process better, making things much easier for you! Doggie toothbrushes come in different sizes and are designed to fit the contour of a canine mouth. Rubber fingertip brushes fit right on one of your

the early stages of any problem so that you can get your dog treatment as soon as possible. You could save your dog's sight!

fingers and have rubber nodes to clean the teeth and massage the gums. This may be easier to handle, as it is akin to rubbing your dog's teeth with your finger.

As with other grooming tasks, accustom your Tibetan Terrier pup to his dental care early on. Start gently, for a few minutes at a time, so that he gets used to the feel of the brush and to your handling his mouth. Offer praise and petting so that he looks at tooth-care time as a time when he gets extra love and attention. The routine should become second nature; he may not like it, but he should at least tolerate it.

Aside from brushing, offer dental toys to your dog and feed crunchy biscuits, which help to minimize plaque. Rope toys have the added benefit of acting like floss as the dog chews. At your adult dog's yearly check-ups, the vet will likely perform a thorough tooth scraping as well as a complete check for any problems. Proper care of your dog's teeth will ensure that you will enjoy your dog's smile for many years to come. The next time your dog goes to give you a hello kiss, you'll be glad you spent the time caring for his teeth.

THE OTHER END

Dogs sometime have troubles with their anal glands, which are sacs located beside the anal vent. These should empty when a dog

has normal bowel movements; if they don't, they can become full or impacted, causing discomfort. Owners often are alarmed to see their dogs scooting across the floor, dragging their behinds behind, this is just a dog's attempt to empty the glands himself.

Some brave owners attempt to evacuate their dogs' anal glands themselves during grooming, but no one will tell you that this is a pleasant task! Thus many owners prefer to make the trip to the vet to have the vet take care of the problem; owners whose dogs visit a groomer can have this done by the groomer if he offers this as part of his services. Regardless, don't neglect the dog's other end in your home-care routine. Look for scooting, licking or other signs of discomfort "back there" to ascertain whether the anal glands need to be emptied.

Your Tibetan Terrier's teeth must be checked and cleaned on a regular basis.

IDENTIFICATION AND TRAVEL

ID FOR YOUR DOG

You love your Tibetan Terrier and want to keep him safe. Of course you take every precaution to prevent his escaping from the yard or becoming lost or stolen. You have a sturdy high fence and you always keep your dog on lead when out and about in public places. If your dog is not properly identified, however, you are overlooking a major aspect of his safety. We hope to never be in a situation where our dog is missing, but we should practice prevention in the unfortunate case that this happens; identification greatly increases the chances of your dog's being returned to you.

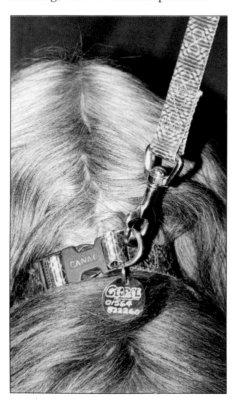

An identification tag is a necessity for every dog. Be sure it is securely fastened to the collar.

There are several ways to identify your dog. First, the traditional dog tag should be a staple in your dog's wardrobe, attached to his everyday collar. Tags can be made of sturdy plastic and various metals and should include your contact information so that a person who finds the dog can get in touch with you right away to arrange his return. Many people today enjoy the wide range of decorative tags available, so have fun and create a tag to match your dog's personality. Of course, it is important that the tag stays on the collar, so have a secure "O" ring attachment; you also can explore the type of tag that slides right onto the collar.

In addition to the ID tag, which every dog should wear even if identified by another method, two other forms of identification have become popular: microchipping and tattooing. In microchipping, a tiny scannable chip is painlessly inserted under the dog's skin. The number is registered to you so that, if your lost dog turns up at a clinic or shelter, the chip can be scanned to retrieve your contact information.

The advantage of the microchip is that it is a permanent form of ID, but there are some factors to consider. Several different companies make microchips, and not all are compatible with the others' scanning devices. It's best to find a company with a universal microchip that can be read by scanners made by other companies as well. It won't do any good to have the dog chipped if the information cannot be retrieved. Also, not every humane society, shelter and clinic is equipped with a scanner, although more and more facilities are equipping themselves. In fact, many shelters microchip dogs that they adopt out to new homes.

In the US, there are five or six major microchip manufacturers as well as a few databases. The American Kennel Club's Companion Animal Recovery unit works in conjunction with HomeAgain™ Companion Animal Retrieval System (Schering-Plough). In the UK, The Kennel Club is affiliated with the National Pet Register, operated by Wood Green Animal Shelters.

Because the microchip is not visible to the eye, the dog must wear a tag that states that he is microchipped so that whoever picks him up will know to have him scanned. He of course also should have a tag with contact information in case his chip cannot be read. Humane societies and veterinary clinics offer this service, which is usually very affordable.

Though less popular than microchipping, tattooing is another permanent method of ID for dogs. Most vets perform this service, and there are also clinics that perform dog tattooing. This is also an affordable procedure and one that will not cause much discomfort for the dog. It is best to put the tattoo in a visible area, such as the ear, to deter theft. It is sad to say that there are cases of dogs' being stolen and sold to research laboratories, but such laboratories will not accept tattooed dogs.

To ensure that the tattoo is effective in aiding your dog's return to you, the tattoo number must be registered with a national organization. That way, when someone finds a tattooed dog a phone call to the registry will quickly match the dog with his owner.

HIT THE ROAD

Car travel with your Tibetan Terrier may be limited to necessity only, such as trips to the vet, or you may bring your dog along almost everywhere you go. This will depend much on your individual dog and how he reacts to rides in the car. You can begin desensitizing your dog to car travel as a pup so that it's something that he's used to. Still, some dogs suffer from motion sickness. Your vet may prescribe a medication for this if trips in the car pose a problem for your dog. At the very least, you will need to get him to the vet, so he will need to tolerate these trips with the least amount of hassle possible.

Start taking your pup on short trips, maybe just around the block to start. If he is fine with short trips, lengthen your rides a little at a time. Start to take him on your errands or just for drives around town. By this time it will be easy to tell whether your dog is a born traveler or would prefer staying at home when you are on the road.

Of course, safety is a concern for dogs in the car. First, he must travel securely, not be left loose to roam about the car where he could be injured or distract the driver. A young pup can be held by a passenger initially but should soon graduate to a travel crate, which can be the same crate he uses in the home. Other options include a car harness (like a seat belt for dogs) and partitioning the back of the car with a gate made for this purpose.

Bring along what you will need for the dog. He should wear his collar and ID tags, of course, and you should bring his leash, water (and food if a long trip) and clean-up materials for potty breaks and in case of motion sickness. Always keep your dog on his leash when you make stops, and never leave him alone in the car. Many a dog has died from the heat inside a closed car; this does not take much time at all. A dog left alone inside a car can also be a target for thieves.

Lightweight wire crates are ideal for traveling with your Tibetans in the car. Never permit your dog to wander freely in a moving vehicle.

TIBETAN TERRIER

BASIC TRAINING PRINCIPLES: PUPPY VS. ADULT

There's a big difference between training an adult dog and training a young puppy. With a young puppy, everything is new. At eight to ten weeks of age, he will be experiencing many things, and he has nothing with which to compare these experiences. Up to this point, he has been with his dam and littermates, not one-on-one with people except in his interactions with his breeder and visitors to the litter.

When you first bring the puppy home, he is eager to please you. This means that he accepts doing things your way. During the next couple of months, he will absorb the basis of everything he needs to know for the rest of his life. This early age is even referred to as the "sponge" stage. After that, for the next 18 months, it's up to you to reinforce good manners by building on the foundation that you've established. Once your puppy is reliable in basic commands and behavior and has reached the appropriate age, you may gradually introduce him to some of the interesting sports, games and activities available to pet owners and their dogs.

Raising your puppy is a family affair. Each member of the family must know what rules to set forth for the puppy and how to use the same one-word commands to mean exactly the same thing every time. Even if yours is a large family, one person will soon be considered by the pup to be the leader, the alpha person in his pack, the "boss" who must be obeyed. Often that highly regarded person turns out to be the one who feeds the puppy. Food ranks very high on the puppy's list of important things! That's why your puppy is rewarded with small

A well-trained dog is a prize-winner to his owner, whether he's a show dog or not! The rewards of training are long-lasting for both dog and owner.

There's a new kid at home and he's ready for school. Be ready to assume the roles of both parent and teacher. At least you don't have to attend PTA meetings and evening conferences.

treats along with verbal praise when he responds to you correctly. As the puppy learns to do what you want him to do, the food rewards are gradually eliminated and only the praise remains. If you were to keep up with the food treats, you could have two problems on your hands—an obese dog and a beggar.

Training begins the minute your Tibetan Terrier puppy steps through the doorway of your home, so don't make the mistake of putting the puppy on the floor and telling him by your actions to "Go for it! Run wild!" Even if this is your first puppy, you

OUR CANINE KIDS

"Everything I learned about parenting, I learned from my dog." How often adults recognize that their parenting skills are mere extensions of the education they acquired while caring for their dogs. Many owners refer to their dogs as their "kids" and treat their canine companions like real members of the family. Surveys indicate that a majority of dog owners talk to their dogs regularly, celebrate their dogs' birthdays and purchase Christmas gifts for their dogs. Another survey shows that dog owners take their dogs to the veterinarian more frequently than they visit their own physicians.

must act as if you know what you're doing: be the boss. An uncertain pup may be terrified to move, while a bold one will be ready to take you at your word and start plotting to destroy the house! Before you collected your puppy, you decided where his own special place would be, and that's where to put him when you first arrive home. Give him a house tour after he has investigated his area and had a nap and a bathroom "pit stop."

It's worth mentioning here that if you've adopted an adult dog that is completely trained to your liking, lucky you! You're off the hook! However, if that dog spent his life up to this point in a kennel, or even in a good home but without any real training, be prepared to tackle the job ahead. A dog three years of age or older with no previous training cannot be blamed for not knowing what he was never taught. While the dog is trying to understand and learn your rules, at the same time he has to unlearn many of his previously self-taught habits and general view of the world.

Working with a professional trainer will speed up your progress with an adopted adult dog. You'll need patience, too. Some new rules may be close to impossible for the dog to accept. After all, he's been successful so far by doing everything his way! (Patience again.) He may agree with your instruction for a few days and then slip back into his

Whether you've adopted a puppy or an adult, the same principles for discipline, positive reinforcement and consistency apply.

BASIC PRINCIPLES OF DOG TRAINING

1. Start training early. A young puppy is ready, willing and able.
2. Timing is your all-important tool. Praise at the exact time that the dog responds correctly. Pay close attention.
3. Patience is almost as important as timing!
4. Repeat! The same word has to mean the same thing every time.
5. In the beginning, praise all correct behavior verbally, along with treats and petting.

needed yet again!) Your dog has to learn to pay attention to your voice, your family, the daily routine, new smells, new sounds and, in some cases, even a new climate.

One of the most important things to find out about a newly adopted adult dog is his reaction to children (yours and others), strangers and your friends, and how he acts upon meeting other dogs. If he was not socialized with dogs as a puppy, this could be a major problem. This does not mean that he's a "bad" dog, a vicious dog or an aggressive dog; rather, it means that he has no idea how to read another dog's body language. There's no way for him to tell whether the other dog is a friend or foe. Survival instinct takes over, telling him to attack first and ask questions later. This definitely calls for professional help and, even then, may not be a behavior that can be corrected 100% reliably (or even at all). If you have a puppy, this is why it is so very important to introduce him properly to other puppies and "dog-friendly" adult dogs.

HOUSE-TRAINING YOUR TIBETAN TERRIER

Dogs are tactility-oriented when it comes to house-training. In other words, they respond to the surface on which they are given approval to eliminate. The choice is yours (the dog's version is in

old ways, so you must be just as consistent and understanding in your teaching as you would be with a puppy. (More patience

THE RIGHT START

The best advice for a potential dog owner is to start with the very best puppy that money can buy. Don't shop around for a bargain in the newspaper. You're buying a companion, not a used car or a second-hand refrigerator. The purchase price of the dog represents a very significant part of the investment, but this is indeed a very small sum compared to the expenses of maintaining the dog in good health. If you purchase a well-bred healthy and sound puppy, you will be starting right. An unhealthy puppy can cost you thousands of dollars in unnecessary veterinary expenses and, possibly, a fortune in heartbreak as well.

won't mean that the dog will soil on every piece of newspaper lying around the house. You are training him to go outside, remember? Starting out by paper-training often is the only choice for a city dog.

WHEN YOUR PUPPY'S "GOT TO GO"
Your puppy's need to relieve himself is seemingly non-stop, but signs of improvement will be seen each week. From 8 to 10 weeks old, the puppy will have to be taken outside every time he wakes up, about 10-15 minutes after every meal and after every period of play—all day long, from first

parentheses): The lawn (including the neighbors' lawns)? A bare patch of earth under a tree (where people like to sit and relax in the summertime)? Concrete steps or patio (all sidewalks, garage and basement floors)? The curbside (watch out for cars)? A small area of crushed stone in a corner of the yard (mine!)? The latter is the best choice if you can manage it because it will remain strictly for the dog's use and is easy to keep clean.

You can start out with paper-training indoors and switch over to an outdoor surface as the puppy matures and gains control over his need to eliminate. For the nay-sayers, don't worry—this

If you don't want your Tibetan Terrier to jump up onto your furniture when he's an adult, you have to train him to keep off at an early age.

An exercise pen will keep your pup confined and safe.

thing in the morning until his bedtime! That's a total of ten or more trips per day to teach the puppy where it's okay to relieve himself. With that schedule in mind, you can see that house-training a young puppy is not a part-time job. It requires someone to be home all day.

If that seems overwhelming or impossible, do a little planning. For example, plan to pick up your puppy at the start of a vacation period. If you can't get home in the middle of the day, plan to hire a dog-sitter or ask a neighbor to come over to take the pup outside, feed him his lunch and then take him out again about ten or so minutes after he's eaten. Also make arrangements with that or another person to be your "emergency" contact if you have to stay late on the job. Remind yourself—repeatedly—that this

hectic schedule improves as the puppy gets older.

HOME WITHIN A HOME

Your Tibetan Terrier puppy needs to be confined to one secure, puppy-proof area when no one is able to watch his every move. Generally the kitchen is the place of choice because the floor is washable. Likewise, it's a busy family area that will accustom the pup to a variety of noises, everything from pots and pans to the telephone, blender and dishwasher. He will also be enchanted by the smell of your cooking (and will never be critical

EXTRA! EXTRA!

The headlines read: "Puppy Piddles Here!" Breeders commonly use newspapers to line their whelping pens, so puppies learn to associate newspapers with relieving themselves. Do not use newspapers to line your pup's crate, as this will signal to your puppy that it is OK to urinate in his crate. If you choose to paper-train your puppy, you will layer newspapers on a section of the floor near the door he uses to go outside. You should encourage the puppy to use the papers to relieve himself, and bring him there whenever you see him getting ready to go. Little by little, you will reduce the size of the newspaper-covered area so that the puppy will learn to relieve himself "on the other side of the door."

CANINE DEVELOPMENT SCHEDULE

It is important to understand how and at what age a puppy develops into adulthood. If you are a puppy owner, consult this Canine Development Schedule to determine the stage of development your puppy is currently experiencing. This knowledge will help you as you work with the puppy in the weeks and months ahead.

PERIOD	AGE	CHARACTERISTICS
FIRST TO THIRD	BIRTH TO SEVEN WEEKS	Puppy needs food, sleep and warmth and responds to simple and gentle touching. Needs mother for security and disciplining. Needs littermates for learning and interacting with other dogs. Pup learns to function within a pack and learns pack order of dominance. Begin socializing pup with adults and children for short periods. Pup begins to become aware of his environment.
FOURTH	EIGHT TO TWELVE WEEKS	Brain is fully developed. Pup needs socializing with outside world. Remove from mother and littermates. Needs to change from canine pack to human pack. Human dominance necessary. Fear period occurs between 8 and 12 weeks. Avoid fright and pain.
FIFTH	THIRTEEN TO SIXTEEN WEEKS	Training and formal obedience should begin. Less association with other dogs, more with people, places and situations. Period will pass easily if you remember this is pup's change-to-adolescence time. Be firm and fair. Flight instinct prominent. Permissiveness and over-disciplining can do permanent damage. Praise for good behavior.
JUVENILE	FOUR TO EIGHT MONTHS	Another fear period about seven to eight months of age. It passes quickly, but be cautious of fright and pain. Sexual maturity reached. Dominant traits established. Dog should understand sit, down, come and stay by now.

NOTE: THESE ARE APPROXIMATE TIME FRAMES. ALLOW FOR INDIVIDUAL DIFFERENCES IN PUPPIES.

LEASH TRAINING

House-training and leash training go hand in hand, literally. When taking your puppy outside to do his business, lead him there on his leash. Unless an emergency potty run is called for, do not whisk the puppy up into your arms and take him outside. If you have a fenced yard, you have the advantage of letting the puppy loose to go out, but it's better to put the dog on the leash and take him to his designated place in the yard until he is reliably house-trained. Taking the puppy for a walk is the best way to house-train a dog. The dog will associate the walk with his time to relieve himself, and the exercise of walking stimulates the dog's bowels and bladder. Dogs that are not trained to relieve themselves on a walk may hold it until they get back home, which of course defeats half the purpose of the walk.

when you burn something). An exercise pen (also called an "ex-pen," a puppy version of a playpen) within the room of choice is an excellent means of confinement for a young pup. He can see out and has a certain amount of space in which to run about, but he is safe from dangerous things like electrical cords, heating units, trash baskets or open kitchen-supply cabinets. Place the pen where the puppy will not get a blast of heat or air conditioning.

In the pen, you can put a few toys, his bed (which can be his crate if the dimensions of pen and crate are compatible) and a few layers of newspaper in one small corner, just in case. A water bowl can be hung at a convenient height on the side of the ex-pen so it won't become a splashing pool for an innovative puppy. His food dish can go on the floor, near but not under the water bowl.

Crates are something that pet owners are at last getting used to for their dogs. Wild or domestic canines have always preferred to sleep in den-like safe spots, and that is exactly what the crate provides. How often have you seen adult dogs that choose to sleep under a table or chair even though they have full run of the house? It's the den connection.

In your "happy" voice, use the word "Crate" every time you put the pup into his den. If he's new to a crate, toss in a small biscuit for him to chase the first few times. At night, after he's been outside, he should sleep in his crate. The crate may be kept in his designated area at night or, if you want to be sure to hear those wake-up yips in the morning, put the crate in a corner of your bedroom. However, don't make any response whatsoever to whining or crying. If he's completely ignored, he'll settle down and get to sleep.

Good bedding for a young puppy is an old folded bath towel or an old blanket, something that is easily washable and disposable if necessary ("accidents" will happen!). Never put newspaper in the puppy's crate. Also those old ideas about adding a clock to replace his mother's heartbeat, or a hot-water bottle to replace her warmth, are just that—old ideas. The clock could drive the puppy nuts, and the hot-water bottle could end up as a very soggy waterbed! An extremely good breeder would have introduced your puppy to the crate by letting two pups sleep together for a couple of nights, followed by several nights alone. How thankful you will be if you found that breeder!

Safe toys in the pup's crate or area will keep him occupied, but monitor their condition closely. Discard any toys that show signs of being chewed to bits. Squeaky parts, bits of stuffing or plastic or any other small pieces can cause intestinal blockage or possibly choking if swallowed.

PROGRESSING WITH POTTY-TRAINING
After you've taken your puppy out and he has relieved himself in the area you've selected, he can have some free time with the family as long as there is someone responsible for watching him. That doesn't mean just someone in the same room who is watching TV or busy on the computer, but one person who is doing nothing other than keeping an eye on the pup, playing with him on the floor and helping him understand his position in the pack.

This first taste of freedom will let you begin to set the house rules. If you don't want the dog on the furniture, now is the time to prevent his first attempts to jump up onto the couch. The word to use in this case is "Off," not "Down." "Down" is the word you will use to teach the down position, which is something entirely different.

Most corrections at this stage come in the form of simply distracting the puppy. Instead of telling him "No" for "Don't chew the carpet," distract the chomping puppy with a toy and he'll forget about the carpet.

The Tibetan Terrier's nose is sensitive enough to seek out his bathroom place even during the snowy winter months.

SMILE WHEN YOU ORDER ME AROUND!

While trainers recommend practicing with your dog every day, it's perfectly acceptable to take a "mental health day" off. It's better not to train the dog on days when you're in a sour mood. Your bad attitude or lack of interest will be sensed by your dog, and he will respond accordingly. Studies show that dogs are well tuned in to their humans' emotions. Be conscious of how you use your voice when talking to your dog. Raising your voice or shouting will only erode your dog's trust in you as his trainer and master.

As you are playing with the pup, do not forget to watch him closely and pay attention to his body language. Whenever you see him begin to circle or sniff, take the puppy outside to relieve himself. If you are paper-training, put him back into his confined area on the newspapers. In either case, praise him as he eliminates while he actually is in the act of relieving himself. Three seconds after he has finished is too late! You'll be praising him for running toward you, picking up a toy or whatever he may be doing at that moment, and that's not what you want to be praising him for. Timing is a vital tool in all dog training. Use it.

Remove soiled newspapers immediately and replace them with clean ones. You may want to take a small piece of soiled paper and place it in the middle of the new clean papers, as the scent will attract him to that spot when it's time to go again. That scent attraction is why it's so important to clean up any messes made in the house by using a product specifically made to eliminate the odor of dog urine and droppings. Regular household cleansers won't do the trick. Pet shops sell the best pet deodorizers. Invest in the largest container you can find.

Scent attraction eventually will lead your pup to his chosen spot outdoors; this is the basis of outdoor training. When you take

"SCHOOL" MODE

When is your puppy ready for a lesson? Maybe not always when you are. Attempting training with treats just before his mealtime is asking for disaster. Notice what times of day he performs best and make that Fido's school time.

your puppy outside to relieve himself, use a one-word command such as "Outside" or "Go-potty" (that's one word to the puppy!) as you attach his leash. Then quickly lead him to his relief spot. You should only carry your pup to the spot if an emergency potty run is required. Now comes the hard part—hard for you, that is. Just stand there until he urinates and defecates. Move him a few feet in one direction or another if he's just sitting there looking at you, but remember that this is neither playtime nor time for a walk. This is strictly a business trip! Then, as he circles and squats (remember your timing!), give him a quiet "Good dog" as praise. If you start to jump for joy, ecstatic over his performance, he'll do one of two things: either he will stop mid-stream, as it were, or he'll do it again for you—in the house—and

expect you to be just as delighted!

Give him five minutes or so and, if he doesn't go in that time, take him back indoors to his confined area and try again in another ten minutes, or immediately if you see him sniffing and circling. By careful observation, you'll soon work out a successful schedule.

Accidents, by the way, are just that—accidents. Clean them up quickly and thoroughly, without comment, after the puppy has been taken outside to finish his business and then put back into his area or crate. If you witness an accident in progress, say "No!" in a stern voice and get the pup outdoors immediately. No punishment is needed. You and your puppy are just learning each other's language, and sometimes it's easy to miss a puppy's message. Chalk it up to experience and watch more closely from now on.

KEEPING THE PACK ORDERLY
Discipline is a form of training that brings order to life. For example, military discipline is what allows the soldiers in an army to work as one. Discipline is a form of teaching and, in dogs, is the basis of how the successful pack operates. Each member knows his place in the pack and all respect the leader, or alpha dog. It is essential for your puppy that you establish this type of

Consistency is an important element in molding your pup's behavior. If you allow him to chew on an object one day, he'll be confused if you forbid him to chew on it the next day.

relationship, with you as the alpha, or leader. It is a form of social coexistence that all canines recognize and accept. Discipline, therefore, is never to be confused with punishment. When you teach your puppy how you want him to behave, and he behaves properly and you praise him for it, you are disciplining him with a form of positive reinforcement.

For a dog, rewards come in the form of praise, a smile, a cheerful tone of voice, a few friendly pats or a rub of the ears. Rewards are also small food treats. Obviously, that does not mean bits of regular dog food. Instead, treats are very small bits of special things like cheese or pieces of soft dog treats. The idea is to reward the dog with something very small that he can taste and swallow, providing instant positive reinforcement. If he has to take time to chew the treat, by the time he is finished he will have forgotten what he did to earn it!

Your puppy should never be physically punished. The displeasure shown on your face and in your voice is sufficient to signal to the pup that he has done something wrong. He wants to please everyone higher up on the social ladder, especially his leader, so a scowl and harsh voice will take care of the error. Growling out the word "Shame!" when the pup is caught in the act of doing something wrong is better than the repetitive "No." Some dogs hear "No" so often that they begin to think it's their name! By the way, do not use the dog's name when you're correcting him. His name is reserved to get his attention for something pleasant about to take place.

There are punishments that have nothing to do with you. For example, your dog may think that chasing cats is one reason for his existence. You can try to stop it as much as you like but without success because it's such fun for the dog. But one good hissing, spitting swipe of a cat's claws across the dog's nose will put an end to the game forever. Intervene only when your dog's eyeball is seriously at risk. Cat scratches can cause permanent damage to an innocent but annoying puppy.

PUPPY KINDERGARTEN

COLLAR AND LEASH
Before you begin your Tibetan Terrier puppy's education, he must be used to his collar and leash. Choose a collar for your

CREATURES OF HABIT

Canine behaviorists and trainers aptly describe dogs as "creatures of habit," meaning that dogs respond to structure in their daily lives and welcome a routine. Do not interpret this to mean that dogs enjoy endless repetition in their training sessions. Dogs get bored just as humans do. Keep training sessions interesting and exciting. Vary the commands and the locations in which you practice. Give short breaks for play in between lessons. A bored student will never be the best performer in the class.

puppy that is secure, but not heavy or bulky. He won't enjoy training if he's uncomfortable. A flat buckle collar is fine for everyday wear and for initial puppy training. For older dogs, there are several types of training collars such as the martingale, which is a double loop that tightens slightly around the neck, or the head collar, which is similar to a horse's halter. Do not use a chain choke collar unless you have been specifically shown how to put it on and how to use it. You may not be disposed to use a chain choke collar even if your breeder has told you that it's suitable for your Tibetan Terrier.

A lightweight 6-foot woven cotton or nylon training leash is preferred by most trainers because it is easy to fold up in your hand and comfortable to hold because there is a certain amount of give to it. There are lessons where the dog will start off 6 feet away from you at the end of the leash. The leash used to take the puppy outside to relieve himself is shorter because you don't want him to roam away from his area. The shorter leash will also be the one to use when you walk the puppy.

If you've been wise enough to enroll in a puppy kindergarten training class, suggestions will be made as to the best collar and leash for your young puppy. I say "wise" because your puppy will be in a class with puppies in his age range (up to five months old) of all breeds and sizes. It's the perfect way for him to learn the right way (and the wrong way) to interact with other dogs as well as their people. You cannot teach your puppy how to interpret another dog's sign language. For a

Puppy kindergarten classes give your Tibetan Terrier pup a chance to interact with other dogs of different breeds.

first-time puppy owner, these socialization classes are invaluable. For experienced dog owners, they are a real boon to further training.

ATTENTION

You've been using the dog's name since the minute you collected

LEADER OF THE PACK

Canines are pack animals. They live according to pack rules, and every pack has only one leader. Guess what? That's you! To establish your position of authority, lay down the rules, and be fair and good-natured in all your dealings with your dog. He will consider young children as his littermates, but the one who trains him, who feeds him, who grooms him, who expects him to come into line, that's his leader. And he who leads must be obeyed.

him from the breeder, so you should be able to get his attention by saying his name—with a big smile and in an excited tone of voice. His response will be the puppy equivalent of "Here I am! What are we going to do?" Your immediate response (if you haven't guessed by now) is "Good dog." Rewarding him at the moment he pays attention to you teaches him the proper way to respond when he hears his name.

EXERCISES FOR A BASIC CANINE EDUCATION

THE SIT EXERCISE

There are several ways to teach the puppy to sit. The first one is to catch him whenever he is about to sit and, as his backside nears the floor, say "Sit, good dog!" That's positive reinforcement and, if your timing is sharp, he will learn that what he's doing at that second is connected to your saying "Sit" and that you think he's clever for doing it!

Another method is to start with the puppy on his leash in front of you. Show him a treat in the palm of your right hand. Bring your hand up under his nose and, almost in slow motion, move your hand up and back so his nose goes up in the air and his head tilts back as he follows the treat in your hand. At that point, he will have to either sit or fall over, so as his back legs buckle under, say

"Sit, good dog," and then give him the treat and lots of praise. You may have to begin with your hand lightly running up his chest, actually lifting his chin up until he sits. Some (usually older) dogs require gentle pressure on their hindquarters with the left hand, in which case the dog should be on your left side. Puppies generally do not appreciate this physical dominance.

After a few times, you should be able to show the dog a treat in the open palm of your hand, raise your hand waist-high as you say "Sit" and have him sit. You thereby will have taught him two things at the same time. Both the verbal command and the motion of the hand are signals for the sit. Your puppy is watching you almost more than he is listening to you, so what you do is just as important as what you say.

Don't save any of these drills only for training sessions. Use them as much as possible at odd times during a normal day. The dog should always sit before being given his food dish. He should sit to let you go through a doorway first, when the doorbell rings or when you stop to speak to someone on the street.

THE DOWN EXERCISE

Before beginning to teach the down command, you must consider how the dog feels about this exercise. To him, "down" is a submissive position. Being flat on the floor with you standing over him is not his idea of fun. It's up to you to let him know that, while it may not be fun, the reward of your approval is worth his effort.

Start with the puppy on your left side in a sit position. Hold the leash right above his collar in your left hand. Have an extra-special treat, such as a small piece of cooked chicken or hot dog, in your right hand. Place it at the end of the pup's nose and steadily move your hand down and forward along the ground. Hold the leash to prevent a sudden lunge for the food. As the puppy goes into the down position, say "Down" very gently.

The difficulty with this exercise is twofold: it's both the submissive aspect and the fact that most people say the word "Down" as if they were drill sergeants in charge of recruits! So issue the command sweetly, give him the treat and have the pup maintain the down position for several seconds. If he tries to get

DOWN

"Down" is a harsh-sounding word and a submissive posture in dog body language, thus presenting two obstacles in teaching the down command. When the dog is about to flop down on his own, tell him "Good down." Pups that are not good about being handled learn better by having food lowered in front of them. A dog that trusts you can be gently guided into position. When you give the command "Down," be sure to say it sweetly!

up immediately, place your hands on his shoulders and press down gently, giving him a very quiet "Good dog." As you progress with this lesson, increase the "down time" until he will hold it until you say "Okay" (his cue for release). Practice this one in the house at various times throughout the day.

By increasing the length of time during which the dog must maintain the down position, you'll find many uses for it. For example, he can lie at your feet in the vet's office or anywhere that both of you have to wait, when you are on the phone, while the family is eating and so forth. If you progress to training for competitive obedience, he'll already be all set for the exercise called the "long down."

THE STAY EXERCISE

You can teach your Tibetan Terrier to stay in the sit, down and stand positions. To teach the sit/stay, have the dog sit on your left side. Hold the leash at waist level in your left hand and let the dog know that you have a treat in your closed right hand. Step forward on your right foot as you say "Stay." Immediately turn and stand directly in front of the dog, keeping your right hand up high so he'll keep his eye on the treat hand and maintain the sit position for a count of five. Return to your original position and offer the reward.

Increase the length of the sit/stay each time until the dog can hold it for at least 30 seconds without moving. After about a week of success, move out on your right foot and take two steps before turning to face the dog. Give the "Stay" hand signal (left palm back toward the dog's head) as you leave. He gets the treat when you return and he holds the sit/stay. Increase the distance that you walk away from him before turning until you reach the length of your training leash. But don't rush it! Go back to the beginning if he moves before he should. No matter what the lesson, never be upset by having to back up for a few days. The repetition and practice are what will make your dog reliable in these commands. It won't do any good to move on to something more difficult if the command is not mastered at the easier levels. Above all, even if you do get frustrated, never let your puppy know! Always keep a positive, upbeat attitude during training, which will transmit to your dog for positive results.

The down/stay is taught in the same way once the dog is completely reliable and steady with the down command. Again, don't rush it. With the dog in the down position on your left side, step out on your right foot as you say "Stay." Return by walking around in back of the dog and into your original position. While you are training, it's okay to murmur something like "Hold on" to encourage him to stay put. When the dog will stay without moving when you are at a distance of 3 or 4 feet, begin to increase the length of time before you return. Be sure he holds the down on your return until you say "Okay." At that

point, he gets his treat—just so he'll remember for next time that it's not over until it's over.

THE COME EXERCISE
No command is more important to the safety of your Tibetan Terrier than "Come." It is what you should say every single time you see the puppy running toward you: "Cespa, come! Good dog." During playtime, run a few feet away from the puppy and turn and tell him to "Come" as he is already running to you. You can go so far as to teach your puppy two things at once if you squat down and hold out your arms. As the pup gets close to you and you're saying "Good dog," bring your right arm in about waist high. Now he's also learning the hand signal, an excellent device should you be on the phone when you need to get him to come to

I WILL FOLLOW YOU
Obedience isn't just a classroom activity. In your home you have many great opportunities to teach your dog polite manners. Allowing your pet on the bed or furniture elevates him to your level, which is not a good idea (the word is "Off!"). Use the "umbilical cord" method, keeping your dog on lead so he has to go with you wherever you go. You sit, he sits. You walk, he heels. You stop, he sit/stays. Everywhere you go, he's with you, but you go first!

Once all basic commands have been reliably learned, handling classes are the next step if you choose to show your Tibetan Terrier. One day you and your Tibetan Terrier could even make it all the way to Best in Show.

Don't make training sessions stressful. Keep them short and positive. Sometimes the TT may not be in the mood for practice, so remember TTs will be TTs!

you. You'll also both be one step ahead when you enter obedience classes.

When the puppy responds to your well-timed "Come," try it with the puppy on the training leash. This time, catch him off guard, while he's sniffing a leaf or watching a bird: "Cespa, come!" You may have to pause for a split second after his name to be sure you have his attention. If the puppy shows any sign of confusion, give the leash a mild jerk and take a couple of steps backward. Do not repeat the command. In this case, you should say "Good come" as he reaches you.

That's the number-one rule of training. Each command word is given just once. Anything more is nagging. You'll also notice that all commands are one word only. Even when they are actually two words, you say them as one.

Never call the dog to come to you—with or without his name—if you are angry or intend to correct him for some misbehavior. When correcting the pup, you go to him. Your dog must always connect "Come" with something pleasant and with your approval; then you can rely on his response.

Puppies, like children, have notoriously short attention spans, so don't overdo it with any of the training. Keep each lesson short. Break it up with a quick run around the yard or a ball toss, repeat the lesson and quit as soon as the pup gets it right. That way, you will always end with a "Good dog."

Life isn't perfect and neither are puppies. A time will come, often around ten months of age, when he'll become "selectively deaf" or choose to "forget" his name. He may respond by wagging his tail (and even seeming to smile at you) with a look that says "Make me!" Laugh, throw his favorite toy and skip the lesson you had planned. Pups will be pups!

THE HEEL EXERCISE

The second most important command to teach, after the come, is the heel. When you are walking your growing puppy, you need to be in control. Besides, it looks terrible to be pulled and yanked down the street, and it's not much fun either. Your eight- to ten-week-old puppy will probably follow you everywhere, but that's his natural instinct, not your control over the situation. However, any time he does follow you, you can say "Heel" and be ahead of the game, as he will learn to associate this command

TIPS FOR TRAINING AND SAFETY

1. Whether on or off leash, practice only in a fenced area.
2. Remove the training collar when the training session is over.
3. Don't try to break up a dogfight.
4. "Come," "Leave it" and "Wait" are safety commands.
5. The dog belongs in a crate or behind a barrier when riding in the car.
6. Don't ignore the dog's first sign of aggression. Aggression only gets worse, so take it seriously.
7. Keep the faces of children and dogs separated.
8. Pay attention to what the dog is chewing.
9. Keep the vet's number near your phone.
10. "Okay" is a useful release command.

with the action of following you before you even begin teaching him to heel.

There is a very precise, almost military, procedure for teaching your dog to heel. As with all other obedience training, begin with the dog on your left side. He will be in a very nice sit and you will have the training leash across your chest. Hold the loop and folded leash in your right hand. Pick up the slack leash above the dog in your left hand and hold it loosely at your side. Step out on your left foot as you say "Heel." If the puppy does not move, give a gentle tug or pat your left leg to get him started. If he surges ahead of you, stop and pull him back gently until he is at your side. Tell him to sit and begin again.

Walk a few steps and stop while the puppy is correctly beside you. Tell him to sit and give mild verbal praise. (More enthusiastic praise will encourage him to think the lesson is over.) Repeat the lesson, increasing the number of steps you take only as long as the dog is heeling nicely beside you. When you end the lesson, have him hold the sit, then give him the "Okay" to let him know that this is the end of the lesson. Praise him so that he knows he did a good job.

The cure for excessive pulling (a common problem) is to stop when the dog is no more than 2

FROM HEEL TO ETERNITY
To begin, step away from the dog, who is in the sit position, on your left foot. That tells the dog you aren't going anywhere. Turn and stand directly in front of him so he won't be tempted to follow. Two seconds is a long, long time to your dog, so increase the time for which he's expected to stay only in short increments. Don't force it. When practicing the heel exercise, your dog will sit at your side whenever you stop. Don't stop for more than three seconds, as your enthusiastic dog will really feel that it's an eternity!

or 3 feet ahead of you. Guide him back into position and begin again. With a really determined puller, try switching to a head collar. This will automatically turn the pup's head toward you so you can bring him back easily to the heel position. Give quiet, reassuring praise every time the leash goes slack and he's staying with you.

Staying and heeling can take a lot out of a dog, so provide playtime and free-running exercise to shake off the stress when the lessons are over. You don't want him to associate training with all work and no fun.

TAPERING OFF TIDBITS
Your dog has been watching you—and the hand that treats— throughout all of his lessons, and

now it's time to break the treat habit. Begin by giving him treats at the end of each lesson only. Then start to give a treat after the end of only some of the lessons. At the end of every lesson, as well as during the lessons, be consistent with the praise. Your pup now doesn't know whether he'll get a treat or not, but he should keep performing well just in case! Finally, you will stop giving treat rewards entirely. Save them for something brand-new that you want to teach him. Keep up the praise and you'll always have a "good dog."

OBEDIENCE CLASSES

It is often said that the Tibetan Terrier is so intelligent that he is prone to asking why he should do something. This means it is up to the owner or handler to convince him of the reasons and benefits, something perhaps more easily said than done!

NO MORE TREATS!
When your dog is responding promptly and correctly to commands, it's time to eliminate treats. Begin by alternating a treat reward with a verbal-praise-only reward. Gradually eliminate all treats while increasing the frequency of praise. Overlook pleading eyes and expectant expressions, but if he's still watching your treat hand, you're on your way to using hand signals.

Most Tibetan Terriers are unlikely ever to be quite so obedient as a highly trained Border Collie for example, but they can still reach very satisfactory standards if their training is approached in the correct way.

The standard of obedience that you can achieve with a Tibetan Terrier will depend very much on how much time you want to devote to training. After a few useful and fairly basic exercises have been achieved, it is often realized that it would indeed be possible to reach greater heights and go on to competition standard. Competitive obedience is certainly not beyond the limits of this breed.

An alert, attentive TT student, ready for obedience school. The structured environment of obedience class offers many advantages to dog and owner.

The advantages of an obedience class are that your dog will have to learn amid the distractions of other people and dogs and that your mistakes will be quickly corrected by the trainer. Teaching your dog along with a qualified instructor and other handlers who may have more dog experience than you is another plus of the class environment. The instructor and other handlers can help you to find the most efficient way of teaching your dog a command or exercise. It's often easier to learn from other people's mistakes than your own. You will also learn all of the requirements for competitive obedience trials, in which you can earn titles and go on to advanced jumping and retrieving exercises, which are fun for many dogs. Obedience classes build the foundation needed for many other canine activities (in which we humans are allowed to participate, too!).

The well-trained Tibetan Terrier will be a welcome guest in many places.

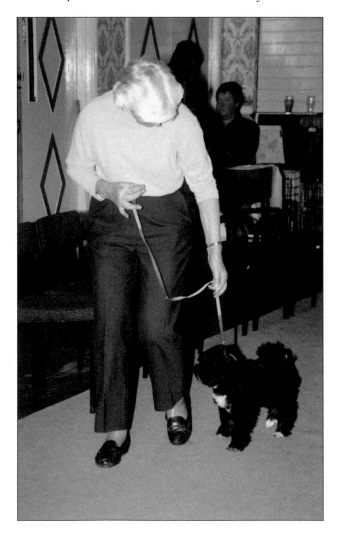

TRAINING FOR OTHER ACTIVITIES

Once your dog has basic obedience under his collar and is 12 months of age, you can enter the world of agility training. Dogs think agility is pure fun, like being turned loose in an amusement park full of obstacles! In addition to agility, there are hunting activities for sporting dogs, lure-coursing events for sighthounds, go-to-ground events for terriers, racing for the Nordic sled dogs, herding trials for the shepherd breeds and tracking, which is open to all "nosey" dogs (which would include all dogs!). For those who like to volunteer, there is the wonderful feeling of owning a therapy dog and visiting hospices, nursing homes and veterans' homes to bring smiles, comfort and companionship to those who live there.

Around the house, your Tibetan Terrier can be taught to

RIGHT CLICK ON YOUR DOG

With three clicks, the dolphin jumps through the hoop. Wouldn't it be nice to have a dog who could obey wordless commands that easily? Clicker training actually was developed by dolphin trainers and today is used on dogs with great success. You can buy a clicker at a pet shop or pet-supply outlet, and then you'll be off and clicking.

You can click your dog into learning new commands, shaping or conditioning his behavior and solving bad habits. The clicker, used in conjunction with a treat, is an extension of positive reinforcement. The dog begins to recognize your happy clicking, and you will never have to rely on any other method. The dog is conditioned to follow your hand with the clicker, just as he would follow your hand with a treat. To discourage the dog from inappropriate behavior (like jumping up or barking), you can use the clicker to set a time frame and then click and reward the dog once he's waited the allotted time without jumping up or barking.

do some simple chores. You might teach him to carry a basket of household items or to fetch the morning newspaper. The kids can teach the dog all kinds of tricks, from playing hide-and-seek to balancing a biscuit on his nose. A family dog is what rounds out the family. Everything he does beyond sitting in your lap or gazing lovingly at you represents the bonus of owning a dog.

Proper training will not only make your Tibetan Terrier an obedient member of your household, but could also lead to a blue ribbon if you decide to show your dog.

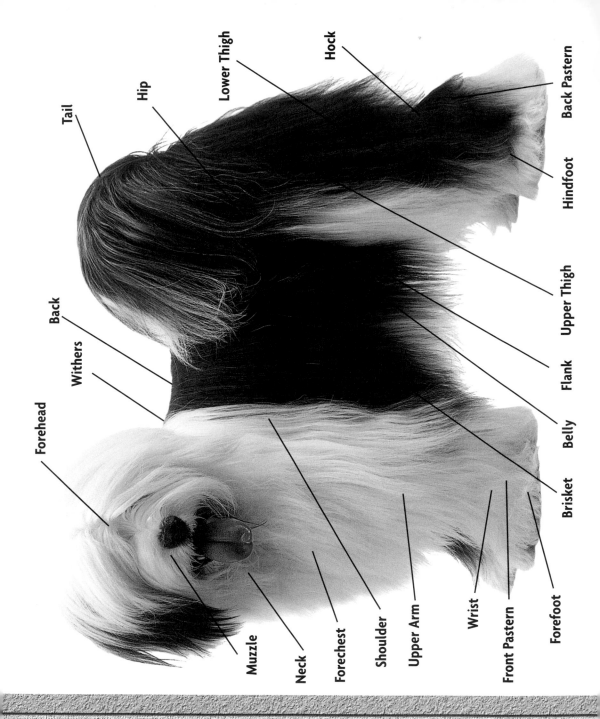

Tail

Lower Thigh

Hock

Back Pastern

Hip

Hindfoot

Upper Thigh

Flank

Back

Withers

Belly

Forehead

Brisket

Forefoot

Front Pastern

Wrist

Upper Arm

Shoulder

Forechest

Neck

Muzzle

PHYSICAL STRUCTURE OF THE TIBETAN TERRIER

HEALTHCARE OF YOUR

TIBETAN TERRIER

By Lowell Ackerman, DVM, DACVD

HEALTHCARE FOR A LIFETIME

When you own a dog, you become his healthcare advocate over his entire lifespan, as well as being the one to shoulder the financial burden of such care. Accordingly, it is worthwhile to focus on prevention rather than treatment, as you and your pet will both be happier.

Of course, the best place to have begun your program of preventive healthcare is with the initial purchase or adoption of your dog. There is no way of guaranteeing that your new furry friend is free of medical problems, but there are some things you can do to improve your odds. You certainly should have done adequate research into the Tibetan Terrier and have selected your puppy carefully rather than buying on impulse. Health issues aside, a large number of pet abandonment and relinquishment cases arise from a mismatch between pet needs and owner expectations. This is entirely preventable with appropriate planning and finding a good breeder.

Regarding healthcare issues specifically, it is very difficult to make blanket statements about where to acquire a problem-free pet, but, again, a reputable breeder is your best bet. In an ideal situation you have the opportunity to see both parents, get references from other owners of the breeder's pups and see genetic-testing documentation for several generations of the litter's ancestors. At the very least, you must thoroughly investigate the Tibetan Terrier and the problems inherent in that breed, as well as the genetic testing available to screen for those problems. Genetic testing offers some important benefits, but testing is available for only a few disorders in a relatively small number of breeds and is not available for some of the most common genetic diseases, such as hip dysplasia, cataracts, epilepsy, cardiomyopathy, etc. This area of research is indeed exciting and increasingly important, and advances will continue to be made each year. In fact, recent research has shown that there is an equivalent dog gene for 75% of known human genes, so research done in either species is likely to benefit the other.

1. Esophagus
2. Lungs
3. Spleen
4. Liver
5. Stomach
6. Intestines
7. Urinary Bladder

INTERNAL ORGANS OF THE TIBETAN TERRIER

We've also discussed that evaluating the behavioral nature of your Tibetan Terrier and that of his immediate family members is an important part of the selection process that cannot be underestimated or overemphasized. It is sometimes difficult to evaluate temperament in puppies because certain behavioral tendencies, such as some forms of aggression, may not be immediately evident. More dogs are euthanized each year for behavioral reasons than for all medical conditions combined, so it is critical to take temperament issues seriously. Start with a well-balanced, friendly companion and put the time and effort into proper socialization, and you will both be rewarded with a lifelong valued relationship.

Assuming that you have started off with a pup from healthy, sound stock, you then become responsible for helping your veterinarian keep your pet healthy. Some crucial things happen before you even bring your puppy home. Parasite control typically begins at two weeks of age, and vaccinations typically begin at six to eight weeks of age. A pre-pubertal evaluation is typically scheduled for about six months of age. At this time, a dental evaluation is done (since the adult teeth are now in), heartworm prevention is started and neutering or spaying is most commonly done.

DENTAL WARNING SIGNS

A veterinary dental exam is necessary if you notice one or any combination of the following in your dog:

- Broken, loose or missing teeth;
- Loss of appetite (which could be due to mouth pain or illness caused by infection);
- Gum abnormalities, including redness, swelling and bleeding;
- Drooling, with or without blood;
- Yellowing of the teeth or gumline, indicating tartar;
- Bad breath.

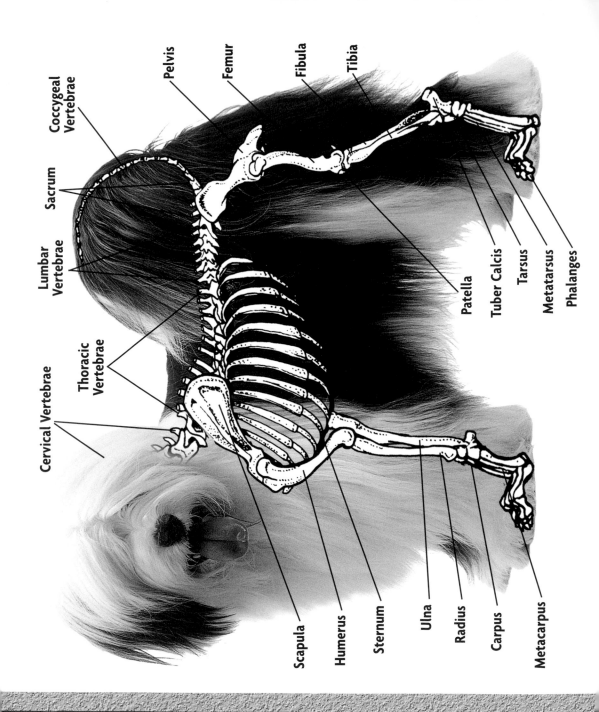

Coccygeal
Vertebrae

Pelvis

Femur

Fibula

Tibia

Sacrum

Patella

Tuber Calcis

Tarsus

Metatarsus

Phalanges

Lumbar
Vertebrae

Thoracic
Vertebrae

Cervical Vertebrae

Scapula

Humerus

Sternum

Ulna

Radius

Carpus

Metacarpus

SKELETAL STRUCTURE OF THE TIBETAN TERRIER

It is critical to commence regular dental care at home if you have not already done so. It may not sound very important, but most dogs have active periodontal disease by four years of age if they don't have their teeth cleaned regularly at home, not just at their veterinary exams. Dental problems lead to more than just bad "doggy breath." Gum disease can have very serious medical consequences. If you start brushing your dog's teeth and using antiseptic rinses from a young age, your dog will be accustomed to it and will not resist. The results will be healthy dentition, which your pet will need to enjoy a long, healthy life.

Most dogs are considered adults at a year of age, although some larger breeds still have some filling out to do up to about two or so years old. Even individual dogs within each breed have different healthcare requirements, so work with your veterinarian to determine what will be needed and what your role should be. This doctor-client relationship is important, because as vaccination guidelines change, there may not be an annual "vaccine visit" scheduled. You must make sure that you see your veterinarian at least annually, even if no vaccines are due, because this is the best opportunity to coordinate health-care activities and to make sure that no medical issues creep by unaddressed.

When your Tibetan Terrier reaches three-quarters of his anticipated lifespan, he is considered a "senior" and likely requires some special care. In general, if you've been taking great care of your canine companion throughout his formative and adult years, the transition to senior status should be a smooth one. Age is not a disease, and as long as everything is functioning as it should, there is no reason why most of late adulthood should not be rewarding for both you and your pet. This is especially true if you have tended to the details, such as regular veterinary visits, proper dental care, excellent nutrition and management of bone and joint issues.

At this stage in your Tibetan Terrier's life, your veterinarian may want to schedule visits twice yearly, instead of once, to run some laboratory screenings, electrocardiograms and the like, and to change the diet to something more digestible. Catching problems early is the best way to manage them effectively. Treating the early stages of heart disease is so much easier than trying to intervene when there is more significant damage to the heart muscle. Similarly, managing the beginning of kidney problems is fairly routine if there is no significant kidney damage. Other problems, like cognitive dysfunction (similar to senility and

Alzheimer's disease), cancer, diabetes and arthritis, are more common in older dogs, but all can be treated to help the dog live as many happy, comfortable years as possible. Just as in people, medical management is more effective (and less expensive) when you catch things early.

SELECTING A VETERINARIAN

There is probably no more important decision that you will make regarding your pet's health-care than the selection of his doctor. Your pet's veterinarian will be a pediatrician, family-practice physician and gerontologist, depending on the dog's life stage, and will be the individual who makes recommendations regarding issues such as when specialists need to be consulted, when diagnostic testing and/or therapeutic intervention is needed and when you will need to seek outside emergency and critical-care services. Your vet will act as your advocate and liaison throughout these processes.

Everyone has his own idea about what to look for in a vet, an individual who will play a big role in his dog's (and, of course, his own) life for many years to come. For some, it is the compassionate caregiver with whom they hope to develop a professional relationship to span the lifetime of their dogs and even their future pets. For others, they are seeking a clinician with keen diagnostic and therapeutic insight who can deliver state-of-the-art healthcare. Still others need a veterinary facility that is open evenings and weekends, is in close proximity or provides mobile veterinary services to accommodate their schedules; these people may not much mind that their dogs might see different veterinarians on each visit. Just as we have different reasons for selecting our own healthcare professionals (e.g., covered by insurance plan, expert in field, convenient location, etc.), we should not expect that there is a one-size-fits-all recommendation for selecting a veterinarian and

INSURANCE FOR YOUR PET

Pet insurance policies are very cost-effective (and very inexpensive by human health-insurance standards), but make sure that you buy the policy long before you intend to use it (preferably starting in puppyhood, because coverage will exclude pre-existing conditions) and that you are actually buying an indemnity insurance plan from an insurance company that is regulated by your state or province. Many insurance policy look-alikes are actually discount clubs that are redeemable only at specific locations and for specific services. An indemnity plan covers your pet at almost all veterinary, specialty and emergency practices and is a great way to manage your pet's ongoing healthcare needs.

veterinary practice. The best advice is to be honest in your assessment of what you expect from a veterinary practice and to conscientiously research the options in your area. You will quickly appreciate that not all veterinary practices are the same, and you will be happiest with one that truly meets your needs.

There is another point to be considered in the selection of veterinary services. Not that long ago, a single veterinarian would attempt to manage all medical and surgical issues as they arose. That was often problematic, because veterinarians are trained in many species and many diseases, and it was just impossible for general veterinary practitioners to be experts in every species, every field and every ailment. However, just as in the human healthcare fields, specialization has allowed general practitioners to concentrate on primary healthcare delivery, especially wellness and the prevention of infectious diseases, and to utilize a network of specialists to assist in the management of conditions that require specific expertise and experience. Thus there are now many types of veterinary specialists, including dermatologists, cardiologists, ophthalmologists, surgeons, internists, oncologists, neurologists, behaviorists, criticalists and others to help primary-care veterinarians deal with complicated

Your Tibetan Terrier relies upon you for his safety, his continued good health and his everyday care and grooming.

medical challenges. In most cases, specialists see cases referred by primary-care veterinarians, make diagnoses and set up management plans. From there, the animals' ongoing care is returned to their primary-care veterinarians. This important team approach to your pet's medical-care needs has provided opportunities for advanced care and an unparalleled level of quality to be delivered.

With all of the opportunities for your Tibetan Terrier to receive high-quality veterinary medical care, there is another topic that needs to be addressed at the same time—cost. It's been said that you can have excellent healthcare or inexpensive healthcare, but never both; this is as true in veterinary medicine as it is in human medicine. While veterinary costs are a fraction of what the same services cost in the human healthcare arena, it is still difficult to

COMMON INFECTIOUS DISEASES

Let's discuss some of the diseases that create the need for vaccination in the first place. Following are the major canine infectious diseases and a simple explanation of each.

Rabies: A devastating viral disease that can be fatal in dogs and people. In fact, vaccination of dogs and cats is an important public-health measure to create a resistant animal buffer population to protect people from contracting the disease. Vaccination schedules are determined on a government level and are not optional for pet owners; rabies vaccination is required by law in all 50 states.

Parvovirus: A severe, potentially life-threatening disease that is easily transmitted between dogs. There are four strains of the virus, but it is believed that there is significant "cross-protection" between strains that may be included in individual vaccines.

Distemper: A potentially severe and life-threatening disease with a relatively high risk of exposure, especially in certain regions. In very high-risk distemper environments, young pups may be vaccinated with human measles vaccine, a related virus that offers cross-protection when administered at four to ten weeks of age.

Hepatitis: Caused by canine adenovirus type 1 (CAV-1), but since vaccination with the causative virus has a higher rate of adverse effects, cross-protection is derived from the use of adenovirus type 2 (CAV-2), a cause of respiratory disease and one of the potential causes of canine cough. Vaccination with CAV-2 provides long-term immunity against hepatitis, but relatively less protection against respiratory infection.

Canine cough: Also called tracheobronchitis, actually a fairly complicated result of viral and bacterial offenders; therefore, even with vaccination, protection is incomplete. Wherever dogs congregate, canine cough will likely be spread among them. Intranasal vaccination with *Bordetella* and parainfluenza is the best safeguard, but the duration of immunity does not appear to be very long, typically a year at most. These are non-core vaccines, but vaccination is sometimes mandated by boarding kennels, obedience classes, dog shows and other places where dogs congregate to try to minimize spread of infection.

Leptospirosis: A potentially fatal disease that is more common in some geographic regions. It is capable of being spread to humans. The disease varies with the individual "serovar," or strain, of *Leptospira* involved. Since there does not appear to be much cross-protection between serovars, protection is only as good as the likelihood that the serovar in the vaccine is the same as the one in the pet's local environment. Problems with *Leptospira* vaccines are that protection does not last very long, side effects are not uncommon and a large percentage of dogs (perhaps 30%) may not respond to vaccination.

Borrelia burgdorferi: The cause of Lyme disease, the risk of which varies with the geographic area in which the pet lives and travels. Lyme disease is spread by deer ticks in the eastern US and western black-legged ticks in the western part of the country, and the risk of exposure is high in some regions. Lameness, fever and inappetence are most commonly seen in affected dogs. The extent of protection from the vaccine has not been conclusively demonstrated.

Coronavirus: This disease has a high risk of exposure, especially in areas where dogs congregate, but it typically causes only mild to moderate digestive upset (diarrhea, vomiting, etc.). Vaccines are available, but the duration of protection is believed to be relatively short and the effectiveness of the vaccine in preventing infection is considered low.

There are many other vaccinations available, including those for *Giardia* and canine adenovirus-1. While there may be some specific indications for their use, and local risk factors to be considered, they are not widely recommended for most dogs.

deal with unanticipated medical costs, especially since they can easily creep into hundreds or even thousands of dollars if specialists or emergency services become involved. However, there are ways of managing these risks. The easiest is to buy pet health insurance and realize that its foremost purpose is not to cover routine healthcare visits but rather to serve as an umbrella for those rainy days when your pet needs medical care and you don't want to worry about whether or not you can afford that care.

VACCINATIONS AND INFECTIOUS DISEASES

There has never been an easier time to prevent a variety of infectious diseases in your dog, but the advances we've made in veterinary medicine come with a price—choice. Now while it may seem that choice is a good thing (and it is), it has never been more difficult for the pet owner (or the veterinarian) to make an informed decision about the best way to protect pets through vaccination.

Years ago, it was just accepted that puppies got a starter series of vaccinations and then annual "boosters" throughout their lives to keep them protected. As more and more vaccines became available, consumers wanted the convenience of having all of that protection in a single injection. The result was "multivalent"

This TT is giving his owner a shout out for his obvious good care.

vaccines that crammed a lot of protection into a single syringe. The manufacturers' recommendations were to give the vaccines annually, and this was a simple enough protocol to follow. However, as veterinary medicine has become more sophisticated and we have started looking more at healthcare quandaries rather than convenience, it became necessary to reevaluate the situation and deal with some tough questions. It is important to realize that whether or not to use a particular vaccine depends on the risk of contracting the disease against which it protects, the severity of the disease if it is contracted, the

duration of immunity provided by
the vaccine, the safety of the
product and the needs of the
individual animal. In a very
general sense, rabies, distemper,
hepatitis and parvovirus are
considered core vaccine needs,
while parainfluenza, *Bordetella
bronchiseptica*, leptospirosis,
coronavirus and borreliosis (Lyme
disease) are considered non-core
needs and best reserved for
animals that demonstrate reason-
able risk of contracting the
diseases.

NEUTERING/SPAYING

Sterilization procedures
(neutering for males/spaying for
females) are meant to accomplish
several purposes. While the
underlying premise is to address
the risk of pet overpopulation,
there are also some medical and
behavioral benefits to the
surgeries as well. For females,
spaying prior to the first estrus
(heat cycle) leads to a marked
reduction in the risk of mammary
cancer. There also will be no
manifestations of "heat" to attract
male dogs and no bleeding in the
house. For males, there is prevention of testicular cancer and a
reduction in the risk of prostate
problems. In both sexes there may
be some limited reduction in
aggressive behaviors toward other
dogs, and some diminishing of
urine marking, roaming and
mounting.

SPAY'S THE WAY

Although spaying a female dog
qualifies as major surgery—an
ovariohysterectomy, in fact—this
procedure is regarded as routine when
performed by a qualified veterinarian
on a healthy dog. The advantages to
spaying a bitch are many and great.
Spayed dogs do not develop uterine
cancer or any life-threatening diseases
of the genitals. Likewise, spayed dogs
are at a significantly reduced risk of
breast cancer. Bitches (and owners) are
relieved of the demands of heat cycles.
A spayed bitch will not leave bloody
stains on your furniture during estrus,
and you will not have to contend with
single-minded macho males trying to
climb your fence in order to seduce
her. The spayed bitch's coat will not
show the ill effects of her estrogen
level's climbing such as a dull,
lackluster outer coat or patches of
hairlessness.

While neutering and spaying
do indeed prevent animals from
contributing to pet overpopulation,
even no-cost and low-cost
neutering options have not
eliminated the problem. Perhaps
one of the main reasons for this is
that individuals that intentionally
breed their dogs and those that
allow their animals to run at large
are the main causes of unwanted
offspring. Also, animals in shelters
are often there because they were
abandoned or relinquished, not

because they came from unplanned matings. Neutering/ spaying is important, but it should be considered in the context of the real causes of animals' ending up in shelters and eventually being euthanized.

One of the important considerations regarding neutering is that it is a surgical procedure. This sometimes gets lost in discussions of low-cost procedures and commoditization of the process. In females, spaying is specifically referred to as an ovariohysterectomy. In this procedure, a midline incision is made in the abdomen and the entire uterus and both ovaries are surgically removed. While this is a major invasive surgical procedure, it usually has few complications because it is typically performed on healthy young animals. However, it is major surgery, as any woman who has had a hysterectomy will attest.

In males, neutering has traditionally referred to castration, which involves the surgical removal of both testicles. While still a significant piece of surgery, there is not the abdominal exposure that is required in the female surgery. In addition, there is now a chemical sterilization option, in which a solution is injected into each testicle, leading to atrophy of the sperm-producing cells. This can typically be done under sedation rather than full anesthesia. This is a relatively new

Neutering can be beneficial regardless of your dog's sex—and it's certainly effective in avoiding unplanned matings.

approach, and there are no long-term clinical studies yet available.

Neutering/spaying is typically done around six months of age at most veterinary hospitals, although techniques have been pioneered to perform the procedures in animals as young as eight weeks of age. In general, the surgeries on the very young animals are done for the specific reason of sterilizing them before they go to their new homes. This is done in some shelter hospitals for assurance that the animals will definitely not produce any pups. Otherwise, these organizations need to rely on owners to comply with their wishes to have the animals "altered" at a later date, something that does not always happen.

There are some exciting immunocontraceptive "vaccines" currently under development, and there may be a time when contraception in pets will not require surgical procedures. We anxiously await these developments.

A scanning electron micrograph of a dog flea, Ctenocephalides canis, on dog hair.

EXTERNAL PARASITES

FLEAS

Fleas have been around for millions of years and, while we have better tools now for controlling them than at any time in the past, there still is little chance that they will end up on an endangered species list. Actually, they are very well adapted to living on our pets, and they continue to adapt as we make advances.

The female flea can consume 15 times her weight in blood during active reproduction and can lay as many as 40 eggs a day. These eggs are very resistant to the effects of insecticides. They hatch into larvae, which then mature and spin cocoons. The immature fleas reside in this pupal stage until the time is right for feeding. This pupal stage is also very resistant to the effects of insecticides, and pupae can last in the environment without feeding for many months. Newly emergent fleas are attracted to animals by the warmth of the animals' bodies, movement and exhaled carbon dioxide. However, when they first emerge from their cocoons, they orient towards light; thus when an animal passes between a flea and the light source, casting a shadow, the flea pounces and starts to feed. If the animal turns out to be a dog or cat, the reproductive cycle continues. If the flea lands on another type of animal, including a person, the flea will bite but will then look for a more appropriate host. An emerging adult flea can survive without feeding for up to 12 months but, once it tastes blood, it can survive off its host for only 3 to 4 days.

It was once thought that fleas spend most of their lives in the environment, but we now know that fleas won't willingly jump off a dog unless leaping to another dog or when physically removed by brushing, bathing or other manipulation. Flea eggs, on the other hand, are shiny and smooth, and they roll off the animal and into the environment. The eggs, larvae and pupae then exist in the environment, but once the adult finds a susceptible animal, it's home sweet home until the flea is forced to seek refuge elsewhere.

Since adult fleas live on the animal and immature forms survive in the environment, a successful treatment plan must address all stages of the flea life cycle. There are now several safe and effective flea-control products that can be applied on a monthly

> ## FLEA PREVENTION FOR YOUR DOG
> - Discuss with your veterinarian the safest product to protect your dog, likely in the form of a monthly tablet or a liquid preparation placed on the back of the dog's neck.
> - For dogs suffering from flea-bite dermatitis, a shampoo or topical insecticide treatment is required.
> - Your lawn and property should be sprayed with an insecticide designed to kill fleas and ticks that lurk outdoors.
> - Using a flea comb, check the dog's coat regularly for any signs of parasites.
> - Practice good housekeeping. Vacuum floors, carpets and furniture regularly, especially in the areas that the dog frequents, and wash the dog's bedding weekly.
> - Follow up house-cleaning with carpet shampoos and sprays to rid the house of fleas at all stages of development. Insect growth regulators are the safest option.

basis. These include fipronil, imidacloprid, selamectin and permethrin (found in several formulations). Most of these products have significant flea-killing rates within 24 hours. However, none of them will control the immature forms in the environment. To accomplish this, there are a variety of insect growth regulators that can be

THE FLEA'S LIFE CYCLE

What came first, the flea or the egg? This age-old mystery is more difficult to comprehend than the actual cycle of the flea. Fleas usually live only about four months. A female can lay 2,000 eggs in her lifetime.

PHOTO BY CAROLINA BIOLOGICAL SUPPLY CO.

Egg

After ten days of rolling around your carpet or under your furniture, the eggs hatch into larvae, which feed on various and sundry debris. In days or months, depending on the climate, the larvae spin cocoons and develop into the pupal or nymph stage, which quickly develop into fleas.

Larva

PHOTO BY CAROLINA BIOLOGICAL SUPPLY CO.

Pupa

These immature fleas must locate a host within 10 to 14 days or they will die. Only about 1% of the flea population exist as adult fleas, while the other 99% exist as eggs, larvae or pupae.

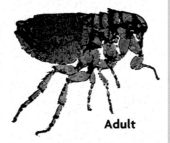

Adult

KILL FLEAS THE NATURAL WAY

If you choose not to go the route of conventional medication, there are some natural ways to ward off fleas:

- Dust your dog with a natural flea powder, composed of such herbal goodies as rosemary, wormwood, pennyroyal, citronella, rue, tobacco powder and eucalyptus.
- Apply diatomaceous earth, the fossilized remains of single-cell algae, to your carpets, furniture and pet's bedding. Even though it's not good for dogs, it's even worse for fleas, which will dry up swiftly and die.
- Brush your dog frequently, give him adequate exercise and let him fast occasionally. All of these activities strengthen the dog's immune system and make him more resistant to disease and parasites.
- Bathe your dog with a capful of pennyroyal or eucalyptus oil.
- Feed a natural diet, free of additives and preservatives. Add some fresh garlic and brewer's yeast to the dog's morning portion, as these items have flea-repelling properties.

sprayed into the environment (e.g., pyriproxyfen, methoprene, fenoxycarb) as well as insect development inhibitors such as lufenuron that can be administered. These compounds have no effect on adult fleas, but they stop immature forms from developing

into adults. In years gone by, we relied heavily on toxic insecticides (such as organophosphates, organochlorines and carbamates) to manage the flea problem, but today's options are not only much safer to use on our pets but also safer for the environment.

TICKS

Ticks are members of the spider class (arachnids) and are blood-sucking parasites capable of transmitting a variety of diseases, including Lyme disease, ehrlichiosis, babesiosis and Rocky Mountain spotted fever. It's easy to see ticks on your own skin, but it is more of a challenge when your furry companion is affected. Whenever you happen to be planning a stroll in a tick-infested area (especially forests, grassy or wooded areas or parks) be prepared to do a thorough inspection of your dog afterward to search for ticks. Ticks can be tricky, so make sure you spend time looking in the cars, between the toes and everywhere else where a tick might hide. Ticks need to be attached for 24–72 hours before they transmit most of the diseases that they carry, so you do have a window of opportunity for some preventive intervention.

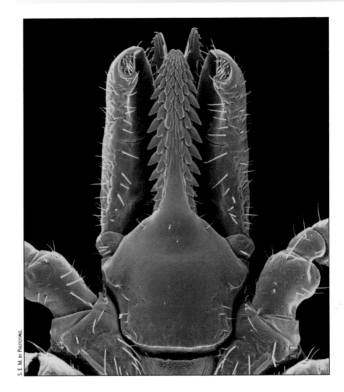

S. E. M. BY PHOTOTAKE.

A TICKING BOMB

There is nothing good about a tick's harpooning his nose into your dog's skin. Among the diseases caused by ticks are Rocky Mountain spotted fever, canine ehrlichiosis, canine babesiosis, canine hepatozoonosis and Lyme disease. If a dog is allergic to the saliva of a female wood tick, he can develop tick paralysis.

Female ticks live to eat and breed. They can lay between 4,000 and 5,000 eggs and they die soon after. Males, on the other hand, live only to mate with the females and continue the process as long as they are able. Most ticks live on multiple hosts before parasitizing dogs. The immature forms typically reside on grass and shrubs, waiting for susceptible animals to walk by. The larvae and nymph stages typically feed on wildlife.

If only a few ticks are present on a dog, they can be plucked out, but it is important to remove the entire head and mouthparts,

A scanning electron micrograph of the head of a female deer tick, *Ixodes dammini*, a parasitic tick that carries Lyme disease.

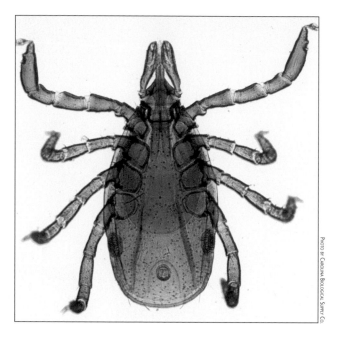

Photo by Carolina Biological Supply Co.

**Deer tick,
Ixodes dammini.**

disposed of in a container of alcohol or household bleach.

Some of the newer flea products, specifically those with fipronil, selamectin and permethrin, have effect against some, but not all, species of tick. Flea collars containing appropriate pesticides (e.g., propoxur, chlorfenvinphos) can aid in tick control. In most areas, such collars should be placed on animals in March, at the beginning of the tick season, and changed regularly. Leaving the collar on when the pesticide level is waning invites the development of resistance. Amitraz collars are also good for tick control, and the active ingredient does not interfere with other flea-control products. The ingredient helps prevent the attachment of ticks to the skin and will cause those ticks already on the skin to detach themselves.

which may be deeply embedded in the skin. This is best accomplished with forceps designed especially for this purpose; fingers can be used but should be protected with rubber gloves, plastic wrap or at least a paper towel. The tick should be grasped as closely as possible to the animal's skin and should be pulled upward with steady, even pressure. Do not squeeze, crush or puncture the body of the tick or you risk exposure to any disease carried by that tick. Once the ticks have been removed, the sites of attachment should be disinfected. Your hands should then be washed with soap and water to further minimize risk of contagion. The tick should be

TICK CONTROL
Removal of underbrush and leaf litter and the thinning of trees in areas where tick control is desired are recommended. These actions remove the cover and food sources for small animals that serve as hosts for ticks. With continued mowing of grasses in these areas, the probability of ticks' surviving is further reduced. A variety of insecticide ingredients (e.g., resmethrin, carbaryl, permethrin, chlorpyrifos, dioxathion and allethrin) are registered for tick control around the home.

MITES

Mites are tiny arachnid parasites that parasitize the skin of dogs. Skin diseases caused by mites are referred to as "mange," and there are many different forms seen in dogs. These forms are very different from one another, each one warranting an individual description.

Sarcoptic mange, or scabies, is one of the itchiest conditions that affects dogs. The microscopic *Sarcoptes* mites burrow into the superficial layers of the skin and can drive dogs crazy with itchiness. They are also communicable to people, although they can't complete their reproductive cycle on people. In addition to being tiny, the mites also are often difficult to find when trying to make a diagnosis. Skin scrapings from multiple areas are examined microscopically but, even then, sometimes the mites cannot be found.

Fortunately, scabies is relatively easy to treat, and there are a variety of products that will successfully kill the mites. Since the mites can't live in the environment for very long without feeding, a complete cure is usually possible within four to eight weeks.

Cheyletiellosis is caused by a relatively large mite, which sometimes can be seen even without a microscope. Often referred to as "walking dandruff," this also causes itching, but not usually as profound as with scabies.

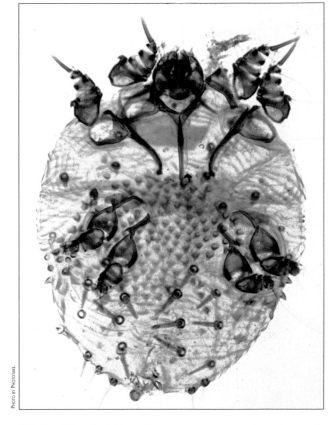

PHOTO BY PHOTOTAKE.

While *Cheyletiella* mites can survive somewhat longer in the environment than scabies mites, they too are relatively easy to treat, being responsive to not only the medications used to treat scabies but also often to flea-control products.

Otodectes cynotis is the canine ear mite and is one of the more common causes of mange, especially in young dogs in shelters or pet stores. That's because the mites are typically present in large numbers and are quickly spread to

Sarcoptes scabiei, commonly known as the "itch mite."

Micrograph of a dog louse, *Heterodoxus spiniger*. Female lice attach their eggs to the hairs of the dog. As the eggs hatch, the larval lice bite and feed on the blood. Lice can also feed on dead skin and hair. This feeding activity can cause hair loss and skin problems.

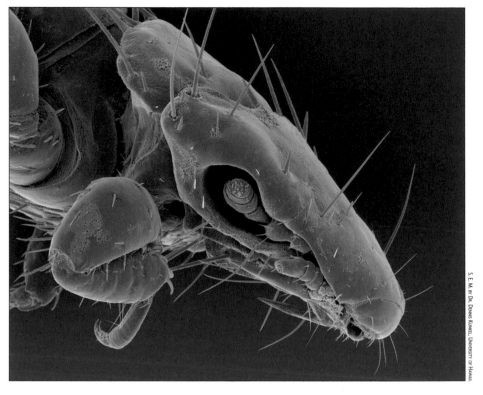

S. E. M. BY DR. DENNIS KUNKEL, UNIVERSITY OF HAWAII.

nearby animals. The mites rarely do much harm but can be difficult to eradicate if the treatment regimen is not comprehensive. While many try to treat the condition with ear drops only, this is the most common cause of treatment failure. Ear drops cause the mites to simply move out of the ears and as far away as possible (usually to the base of the tail) until the insecticide levels in the ears drop to an acceptable level—then it's back to business as usual! The successful treatment of ear mites requires treating all animals in the household with a systemic insecti-

cide, such as selamectin, or a combination of miticidal ear drops combined with whole-body flea-control preparations.

Demodicosis, sometimes referred to as red mange, can be one of the most difficult forms of mange to treat. Part of the problem has to do with the fact that the mites live in the hair follicles and they are relatively well shielded from topical and systemic products. The main issue, however, is that demodectic mange typically results only when there is some underlying process interfering with the dog's immune system.

Since *Demodex* mites are normal residents of the skin of mammals, including humans, there is usually a mite population explosion only when the immune system fails to keep the number of mites in check. In young animals, the immune deficit may be transient or may reflect an actual inherited immune problem. In older animals, demodicosis is usually seen only when there is another disease hampering the immune system, such as diabetes, cancer, thyroid problems or the use of immune-suppressing drugs. Accordingly, treatment involves not only trying to kill the mange mites but also discerning what is interfering with immune function and correcting it if possible.

Chiggers represent several different species of mite that don't parasitize dogs specifically, but do latch on to passersby and can cause irritation. The problem is most prevalent in wooded areas in the late summer and fall. Treatment is not difficult, as the mites do not complete their life cycle on dogs and are susceptible to a variety of miticidal products.

Mosquitoes

Mosquitoes have long been known to transmit a variety of diseases to people, as well as just being biting pests during warm weather. They also pose a real risk to pets. Not only

ILLUSTRATION BY PHOTOTAKE

do they carry deadly heartworms but recently there also has been much concern over their involvement with West Nile virus. While we can avoid heartworm with the use of preventive medications, there are no such preventives for West Nile virus. The only method of prevention in endemic areas is active mosquito control. Fortunately, most dogs that have been exposed to the virus only developed flu-like symptoms and, to date, there have not been the large number of reported deaths in canines as seen in some other species.

Illustration of *Demodex folliculoram.*

MOSQUITO REPELLENT
Low concentrations of DEET (less than 10%), found in many human mosquito repellents, have been safely used in dogs but, in these concentrations, probably give only about two hours of protection. DEET may be safe in these small concentrations, but since it is not licensed for use on dogs, there is no research proving its safety for dogs. Products containing permethrin give the longest-lasting protection, perhaps two to four weeks. As DEET is not licensed for use on dogs, and both DEET and permethrin can be quite toxic to cats, appropriate care should be exercised. Other products, such as those containing oil of citronella, also have some mosquito-repellent activity, but typically have a relatively short duration of action.

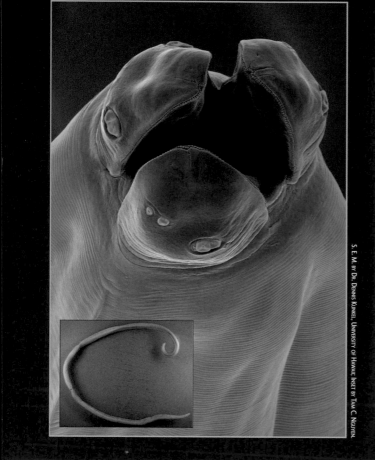

ASCARID DANGERS

The most commonly encountered worms in dogs are roundworms known as ascarids. *Toxascaris leonine* and *Toxocara canis* are the two species that infect dogs. Subsisting in the dog's stomach and intestines, adult roundworms can grow to 7 inches in length and adult females can lay in excess of 200,000 eggs in a single day.

In humans, visceral larval migrans affects people who have ingested eggs of *Toxocara canis*, which frequently contaminates children's sandboxes, beaches and park grounds. The roundworms reside in the human's stomach and intestines, as they would in a dog's, but do not mature. Instead, they find their way to the liver, lungs and skin, or even to the heart or kidneys in severe cases. Deworming puppies is critical in preventing the infection in humans, and young children should never handle nursing pups who have not been dewormed.

The ascarid roundworm *Toxocara canis*, showing the mouth with three lips. INSET: Photomicrograph of the roundworm *Ascaris lumbricoides*.

INTERNAL PARASITES: WORMS

ASCARIDS

Ascarids are intestinal roundworms that rarely cause severe disease in dogs. Nonetheless, they are of major public health significance because they can be transferred to people. Sadly, it is children who are most commonly affected by the parasite, probably from inadvertently ingesting ascarid-contaminated soil. In fact, many yards and children's sandboxes contain appreciable numbers of ascarid eggs. So, while ascarids don't bite dogs or latch onto their intestines to suck blood, they do cause some nasty medical conditions in children and are best eradicated from our furry friends. Because pups can start passing ascarid eggs by three weeks of age, most parasite-control programs begin at two weeks of age and are repeated every two weeks until pups are eight weeks old. It is important to

HOOKED ON ANCYLOSTOMA

Adult dogs can become infected by the bloodsucking nematodes we commonly call hookworms via ingesting larvae from the ground or via the larvae penetrating the dog's skin. It is not uncommon for infected dogs to show no symptoms of hookworm infestation. Sometimes symptoms occur within ten days of exposure. These symptoms can include bloody diarrhea, anemia, loss of weight and general weakness. Dogs pass the hookworm eggs in their stools, which serves as the vet's method of identifying the infestation. The hookworm larvae can encyst themselves in the dog's tissues and be released when the dog is experiencing stress.

Caused by an *Ancylostoma* species whose common host is the dog, cutaneous larval migrans affects humans, causing itching and lumps and streaks beneath the surface of the skin.

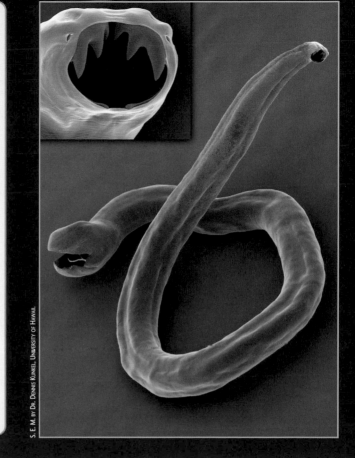

S. E. M. BY DR. DENNIS KUNKEL, UNIVERSITY OF HAWAII.

realize that bitches can pass ascarids to their pups even if they test negative prior to whelping. Accordingly, bitches are best treated at the same time as the pups.

HOOKWORMS

Unlike ascarids, hookworms do latch onto a dog's intestinal tract and can cause significant loss of blood and protein. Similar to ascarids, hookworms can be transmitted to humans, where they cause a condition known as cutaneous larval migrans. Dogs can become infected either by consuming the infective larvae or by the larvae's penetrating the skin directly. People most often get infected when they are lying on the ground (such as on a beach) and the larvae penetrate the skin. Yes, the larvae can penetrate through a beach blanket. Hookworms are typically susceptible to the same medications used to treat ascarids.

The hookworm *Ancylostoma caninum* infests the intestines of dogs. INSET: Note the row of hooks at the posterior end, used to anchor the worm to the intestinal wall.

WHIPWORMS

Whipworms latch onto the lower aspects of the dog's colon and can cause cramping and diarrhea. Eggs do not start to appear in the dog's feces until about three months after the dog was infected. This worm has a peculiar life cycle, which makes it more difficult to control than ascarids or hookworms. The good thing is that whipworms rarely are transferred to people.

Some of the medications used to treat ascarids and hookworms are also effective against whipworms, but, in general, a separate treatment protocol is needed. Since most of the medications are effective against the adults but not the eggs or larvae, treatment is typically repeated in three weeks, and then often in three

Adult whipworm, *Trichuris* sp., an intestinal parasite.

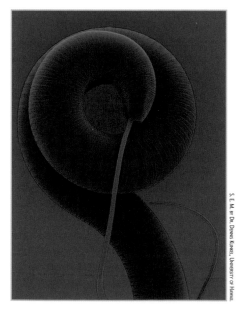

S. E. M. BY DR. DENNIS KUNKEL, UNIVERSITY OF HAWAII.

WORM-CONTROL GUIDELINES

- Practice sanitary habits with your dog and home.
- Clean up after your dog and don't let him sniff or eat other dogs' droppings.
- Control insects and fleas in the dog's environment. Fleas, lice, cockroaches, beetles, mice and rats can act as hosts for various worms.
- Prevent dogs from eating uncooked meat, raw poultry and dead animals.
- Keep dogs and children from playing in sand and soil.
- Kennel dogs on cement or gravel; avoid dirt runs.
- Administer heartworm preventives regularly.
- Have your vet examine your dog's stool at your annual visits.
- Select a boarding kennel carefully so as to avoid contamination from other dogs or an unsanitary environment.
- Prevent dogs from roaming. Obey local leash laws.

months as well. Unfortunately, since dogs don't develop resistance to whipworms, it is difficult to prevent them from getting reinfected if they visit soil contaminated with whipworm eggs.

TAPEWORMS

There are many different species of tapeworm that affect dogs, but *Dipylidium caninum* is probably the most common and is spread by fleas. Flea larvae feed on organic debris and tapeworm eggs in the environment and, when a dog chews at himself and manages to ingest fleas, he might get a dose of tapeworm at the same time. The tapeworm then develops further in the intestine of the dog.

The tapeworm itself, which is a parasitic flatworm that latches onto the intestinal wall, is composed of numerous segments. When the segments break off into the intestine (as proglottids), they may accumulate around the rectum, like grains of rice. While this tapeworm is disgusting in its behavior, it is not directly communicable to humans (although humans can also get infected by swallowing fleas).

A much more dangerous flatworm is *Echinococcus multilocularis*, which is typically found in foxes, coyotes and wolves. The eggs are passed in the feces and infect rodents, and, when dogs eat the rodents, the dogs can be infected by thousands of adult tapeworms. While the parasites don't cause many problems in dogs, this is considered the most lethal worm infection that people can get. Take appropriate precautions if you live in an area in which these tapeworms are found. Do not use mulch that may contain feces of dogs, cats or wildlife, and discourage your pets from hunting wildlife. Treat these tapeworm infections aggressively in pets, because if humans get infected, approximately half die.

HEARTWORMS

Heartworm disease is caused by the parasite *Dirofilaria immitis* and is seen in dogs around the world. A member of the roundworm group, it is spread between dogs by the bite of an infected mosquito. The mosquito injects infective larvae into the dog's skin with its bite, and these larvae develop under the skin for a period of time before making their way to the heart. There they develop into adults, which grow and create blockages of the heart, lungs and major blood vessels there. They also start producing offspring (microfilariae)

A dog tapeworm proglottid (body segment).

The dog tapeworm *Taenia pisiformis.*

S. E. M. BY DR. DENNIS KUNKEL, UNIVERSITY OF HAWAII.

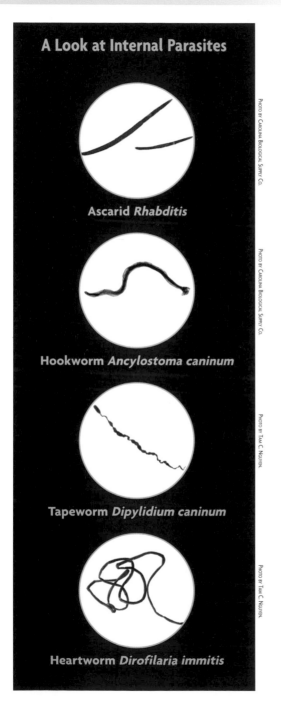

A Look at Internal Parasites

Ascarid *Rhabditis*

Hookworm *Ancylostoma caninum*

Tapeworm *Dipylidium caninum*

Heartworm *Dirofilaria immitis*

Photo by Carolina Biological Supply Co.

Photo by Carolina Biological Supply Co.

Photo by Tam C. Nguyen

Photo by Tam C. Nguyen

and these microfilariae circulate in the bloodstream, waiting to hitch a ride when the next mosquito bites. Once in the mosquito, the microfilariae develop into infective larvae and the entire process is repeated.

When dogs get infected with heartworm, over time they tend to develop symptoms associated with heart disease, such as coughing, exercise intolerance and potentially many other manifestations. Diagnosis is confirmed by either seeing the microfilariae themselves in blood samples or using immunologic tests (antigen testing) to identify the presence of adult heartworms. Since antigen tests measure the presence of adult heartworms and microfilarial tests measure offspring produced by adults, neither are positive until six to seven months after the initial infection. However, the beginning of damage can occur by fifth-stage larvae as early as three months after infection. Thus it is possible for dogs to be harboring problem-causing larvae for up to three months before either type of test would identify an infection.

The good news is that there are great protocols available for preventing heartworm in dogs. Testing is critical in the process, and it is important to understand the benefits as well as the limitations of such testing. All dogs six months of age or older that have not been on continuous heartworm-preventive medication should be

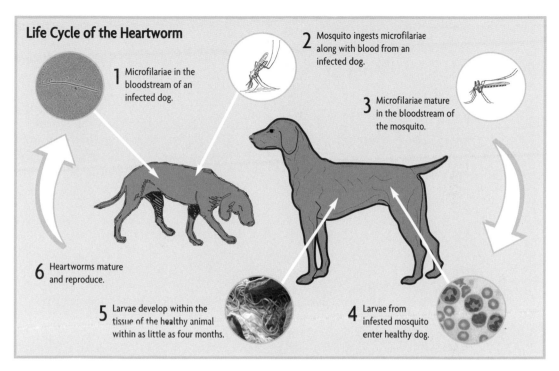

Life Cycle of the Heartworm

1 Microfilariae in the bloodstream of an infected dog.

2 Mosquito ingests microfilariae along with blood from an infected dog.

3 Microfilariae mature in the bloodstream of the mosquito.

4 Larvae from infested mosquito enter healthy dog.

5 Larvae develop within the tissue of the healthy animal within as little as four months.

6 Heartworms mature and reproduce.

screened with microfilarial or antigen tests. For dogs receiving preventive medication, periodic antigen testing helps assess the effectiveness of the preventives. The American Heartworm Society guidelines suggest that annual retesting may not be necessary when owners have absolutely provided continuous heartworm prevention. Retesting on a two- to three-year interval may be sufficient in these cases. However, your veterinarian will likely have specific guidelines under which heartworm preventives will be prescribed, and many prefer to err on the side of safety and retest annually.

It is indeed fortunate that heartworm is relatively easy to prevent, because treatments can be as life-threatening as the disease itself. Treatment requires a two-step process that kills the adult heartworms first and then the microfilariae. Prevention is obviously preferable; this involves a once-monthly oral or topical treatment. The most common oral preventives include ivermectin (not suitable for some breeds), moxidectin and milbemycin oxime; the once-a-month topical drug selamectin provides heartworm protection in addition to flea, tick and other parasite controls.

TIBETAN TERRIER

Is dog showing in your blood? Are you excited by the idea of gaiting your handsome Tibetan Terrier around the ring to the thunderous applause of an enthusiastic audience? Are you certain that your beloved Tibetan Terrier is flawless? You are not alone! Every loving owner thinks that his dog has no faults, or too few to mention. No matter how many times an owner reads the breed standard, he cannot find any faults in his aristocratic companion dog. If this sounds like you, and if you are considering entering your Tibetan Terrier in a dog show, here are some basic questions to ask yourself:

- Did you purchase a "show-quality" puppy from the breeder?
- Is your puppy at least six months of age?
- Does the puppy exhibit correct show type for his breed?
- Does your puppy have any disqualifying faults?
- Is your Tibetan Terrier registered with the American Kennel Club?
- How much time do you have to devote to training, grooming, conditioning and exhibiting your dog?

- Do you understand the rules and regulations of a dog show?
- Do you have time to learn how to show your Tibetan Terrier properly?
- Do you have the financial resources to invest in showing your dog?
- Will you show the dog yourself or hire a professional handler?
- Do you have a vehicle that can accommodate your weekend trips to the dog shows?

FOR MORE INFORMATION...

For reliable up-to-date information about registration, dog shows and other canine competitions, contact one of the national registries by mail or via the Internet.

American Kennel Club
5580 Centerview Dr., Raleigh, NC 27606-3390
www.akc.org

United Kennel Club
100 E. Kilgore Road, Kalamazoo, MI 49002
www.ukcdogs.com

Canadian Kennel Club
89 Skyway Ave., Suite 100, Etobicoke, Ontario
M9W 6R4 Canada
www.ckc.ca

The Kennel Club
1-5 Clarges St., Piccadilly, London W1Y 8AB, UK
www.the-kennel-club.org.uk

Preparing for the show ring, here's a backstage look at the grooming area and a Tibetan Terrier being readied for the ring.

Success in the show ring requires more than a pretty face, a waggy tail and a pocketful of liver. Even though dog shows can be exciting and enjoyable, the sport of conformation makes great demands on the exhibitors and the dogs. Winning exhibitors live for their dogs, devoting time and money to their dogs' presentation, conditioning and training. Very few novices, even those with good dogs, will find themselves in the winners' circle, though it does happen. Don't be disheartened, though. Every exhibitor began as a novice and worked his way up to the Group ring. It's the "working your way up" part that you must keep in mind.

Assuming that you have purchased a puppy of the correct type and quality for showing, let's begin to examine the world of showing and what's required to get started. Although the entry fee into a dog show is nominal, there are lots of other hidden costs involved with "finishing" your Tibetan Terrier, that is, making him a champion. Things like equipment, travel, training and conditioning all cost money. A more serious campaign will include fees for a professional handler, boarding, cross-country travel and advertising. Top-winning show dogs can represent a very considerable investment— over $100,000 has been spent in campaigning some dogs. (The investment can be less, of course, for owners who don't use professional handlers.)

Many owners, on the other hand, enter their "average" Tibetan Terriers in dog shows for the fun and enjoyment of it. Dog showing makes an absorbing hobby, with many rewards for dogs and owners alike. If you're having fun, meeting other people who share your interests and enjoying the overall experience, you likely will catch the "bug." Once the dog-show bug bites, its effects can last a lifetime; it's certainly much better than a deer tick! Soon you will be envisioning yourself in the center ring at the Westminster Kennel Club Dog Show in New York City, competing for the prestigious Best in Show cup. This magical dog show is televised annually from Madison Square Garden, and the victorious dog becomes a celebrity overnight.

AKC CONFORMATION SHOWING

GETTING STARTED
Visiting a dog show as a spectator is a great place to start. Pick up the show catalog to find out what time your breed is being shown, who is judging the breed and in which ring the classes will be held. To start, Tibetan Terriers compete against other Tibetan Terriers, and the winner is selected as Best of Breed by the judge. This is the procedure for each breed. At a group show, all of the Best of Breed winners go on

Exhibitors are expected to follow the judge's instructions to a "T." This judge is instructing her exhibitors to begin gaiting the dogs.

DRESS THE PART

It's a dog show, so don't forget your costume. Even though the show is about the dog, you also must play your role well. You have been cast as the "dog handler" and you must smartly dress the part. Solid colors make a nice complement to the dog's coat, but choose colors that contrast. You don't want to be wearing a solid color that blends mostly or entirely with the major or only color of your dog. Whether the show is indoors or out, you still must dress properly. You want the judge to perceive you as being professional, so polish, polish, polish! And don't forget to wear sensible shoes; remember, you have to gait around the ring with your dog.

to compete for Group One in their respective group. For example, all Best of Breed winners in a given group compete against each other; this is done for all seven groups. Finally, all seven group winners go head to head in the ring for the Best in Show award.

What most spectators don't understand is the basic idea of conformation. A dog show is often referred to as a "conformation" show. This means that the judge should decide how each dog stacks up (conforms) to the breed standard for his given breed: how well does this Tibetan Terrier conform to the ideal representative detailed in the standard?

Ideally, this is what happens. In reality, however, this ideal often gets slighted as the judge compares Tibetan Terrier #1 to Tibetan Terrier #2. Again, the ideal is that each dog is judged based on his merits in comparison to his breed standard, not in comparison to the other dogs in the ring. It is easier for judges to compare dogs of the same breed to decide which they think is the better specimen; in the Group and Best in Show ring, however, it is very difficult to compare one breed to another, like apples to oranges. Thus the dog's conformation to the breed standard—not to mention advertising dollars and good handling—is essential to success in conformation shows. The dog described in the standard (the standard for each AKC breed is written and approved by the breed's national parent club and then submitted to the AKC for

The Tibetan Terrier's gait reveals much about his sound structure, including his hindquarter assembly and the flatness of his feet.

approval) is the perfect dog of that breed, and breeders keep their eye on the standard when they choose which dogs to breed, hoping to get closer and closer to the ideal with each litter.

Another good first step for the novice is to join a dog club. You will be astonished by the many and different kinds of dog clubs in the country, with about 5,000 clubs holding events every year. Most clubs require that prospective new members present two letters of recommendation from existing members. Perhaps you've made some friends visiting a show held by a particular club and you would like to join that club. Dog clubs may specialize in a single breed, like a local or

regional Tibetan Terrier club, or in a specific pursuit, such as obedience, tracking or hunting tests. There are all-breed clubs for all-dog enthusiasts; they sponsor special training days, seminars on topics like grooming or handling or lectures on breeding or canine genetics. There are also clubs that specialize in certain types of dogs, like herding dogs, hunting dogs, companion dogs, etc.

A parent club is the national organization, sanctioned by the AKC, which promotes and safeguards its breed in the country. The Tibetan Terrier Club of America, Inc. was formed in 1957 and can be contacted on the Internet at www.ttca-online.org. The parent club holds an annual

The group judging is underway as the Non-Sporting Dogs are lined up for the judge's evaluation.

national specialty show, usually in a different city each year, in which many of the country's top dogs, handlers and breeders gather to compete. At a specialty show, only members of a single breed are invited to participate. There are also group specialties, in which all members of a group are invited. For more information about dog clubs in your area, contact the AKC at www.akc.org on the Internet or write them at their Raleigh, NC address.

HOW SHOWS ARE ORGANIZED

Three kinds of conformation shows are offered by the AKC. There is the all-breed show, in which all AKC-recognized breeds can compete; the specialty show, which is for one breed only and usually sponsored by the breed's parent club; and the group show, for all breeds in one of the AKC's seven groups. The Tibetan Terrier competes in the Non-Sporting Group.

For a dog to become an AKC champion of record, the dog must earn 15 points at shows. The points must be awarded by at least three different judges and must include two "majors" under different judges. A "major" is a three-, four- or five-point win, and the number of points per win is determined by the number of dogs competing in the show on that day. (Dogs that are absent or are excused are not counted.) The

number of points that are awarded varies from breed to breed. More dogs are needed to attain a major in more popular breeds, and fewer dogs are needed in less popular breeds. Yearly, the AKC evaluates the number of dogs in competition in each division (there are 14 divisions in all, based on geography) and may or may not change the number of dogs required for each number of points. For example, a major in Division 2 (Delaware, New Jersey and Pennsylvania) recently required 17 dogs or 16 bitches for a three-point major, 29 dogs or 27 bitches for a four-point major and 51 dogs or 46 bitches for a five-point major. The Tibetan Terrier attracts numerically proportionate representation at all-breed shows.

Only one dog and one bitch of each breed can win points at a given show. There are no "co-ed" classes except for champions of record. Dogs and bitches do not compete against each other until

The judge will check the dog's mouth to check for a proper bite and strong evenly placed teeth.

they are champions. Dogs that are not champions (referred to as "class dogs") compete in one of five classes. The class in which a dog is entered depends on age and previous show wins. First there is the Puppy Class (sometimes divided further into classes for 6- to 9-month-olds and 9- to 12-month-olds); next is the Novice Class (for dogs that have no points toward their championship and whose only first-place wins have come in the Puppy Class or the Novice Class, the latter class limited to three first places); then there is the American-bred Class (for dogs bred in the US); the Bred-by-Exhibitor Class (for dogs handled by their breeders or by immediate family members of

their breeders) and the Open Class (for any non-champions). Any dog may enter the Open Class, regardless of age or win history, but to be competitive the dog should be older and have ring experience.

The judge at the show begins judging the male dogs in the Puppy Class(es) and proceeds through the other classes. The judge awards first through fourth place in each class. The first-place winners of each class then compete with one another in the Winners Class to determine Winners Dog. The judge then starts over with the bitches, beginning with the Puppy Class(es) and proceeding up to the Winners Class to award Winners Bitch, just as he did with the

Gaiting the dog on a taut lead gives the handler better control of the dog's speed and movement.

dogs. A Reserve Winners Dog and Reserve Winners Bitch are also selected; they could be awarded the points in the case of a disqualification.

The Winners Dog and Winners Bitch are the two that are awarded the points for their breed. They then go on to compete with any champions of record (often called "specials") of their breed that are entered in the show. The champions may be dogs or bitches; in this class, all are shown together. The judge reviews the Winners Dog and Winners Bitch along with all of the champions to select the Best of Breed winner. The Best of Winners is selected between the Winners Dog and Winners Bitch; if one of these two is selected Best of Breed as well, he or she is automatically determined Best of Winners. Lastly, the judge selects Best of Opposite Sex to the Best of Breed winner. The Best of Breed winner then goes on to the Group competition.

At a Group or all-breed show, the Best of Breed winners from each breed are divided into their respective groups to compete against one another for Group One through Group Four. Group One (first place) is awarded to the dog that best lives up to the ideal for his breed as described in the standard. A Group judge, therefore, must have a thorough working knowledge of many breed

Ch. Sim-Pa Lea's Razzmatazz, handled by breeder David Murray, was the number-one Tibetan Terrier in 2001 and ranked among the top Non-Sporting Dogs for three years.

standards. After placements have been made in each Group, the seven Group One winners (from the Sporting Group, Toy Group, Hound Group, etc.) compete against each other for the top honor, Best in Show.

There are different ways to find out about dog shows in your area. The American Kennel Club's monthly magazine, the *American Kennel Gazette,* is accompanied by the *Events Calendar*; this magazine is available through subscription. You can also look on the AKC's and your parent club's websites for information and check the event listings in your local newspaper.

Your Tibetan Terrier must be six months of age or older and registered with the AKC in order to be entered in AKC-sanctioned shows in which there are classes

In the breed or group ring, the TT is surely a show dog on the move!

for the Tibetan Terrier. Your Tibetan Terrier also must not possess any disqualifying faults and must be sexually intact. The reason for the latter is simple: dog shows are the proving grounds to determine which dogs and bitches are worthy of being bred. If they cannot be bred, that defeats the purpose! On that note, only dogs that have achieved championships, thus proving their excellent quality, should be bred. If you have spayed or neutered your dog, however, there are many AKC events other than conformation, such as obedience trials, agility trials and the Canine Good Citizen® Program, in which you and your Tibetan Terrier can participate.

YOU'RE AT THE SHOW, NOW WHAT?
You will fill out an entry form when you register for the show. You must decide and designate on the form in which class you will enter your puppy or adult dog. Remember that some classes are more competitive than others and have limitations based on age and win history. Hopefully you will not be in the first class of the day so you can take some time watching exactly how the judge is conducting the ring. Notice how the handlers are stacking their dogs, meaning setting them up. Does the judge prefer the dogs to be facing one direction or another? Take special note as to how the judge is moving the dogs and how he is instructing the

ON THE MOVE

The truest test of a dog's proper structure is his gait, the way the dog moves. The American Kennel Club defines gait as "the pattern of footsteps at various rates of speed, each pattern distinguished by a particular rhythm and footfall." That the dog moves smoothly and effortlessly indicates to the judge that the dog's structure is well made. From the four-beat gallop, the fastest of canine gaits, to the high-lifting hackney gait, each breed varies in its correct gait; not every breed is expected to move in the same way. Each breed standard defines the correct gait for its breed and often identifies movement faults, such as toeing in, side-winding, over-reaching or crossing over.

interfere with the other dogs. The judge's first direction, usually, is for all of the handlers to "take the dogs around," which means that everyone gaits his dog around the periphery of the ring.

While you're in the ring, don't let yourself (or your dog) become distracted. Concentrate on your dog; he should have your full attention. Stack him in the best way possible. Teach him to free-stand while you hold a treat out for him. Let him understand that he must hold this position for at least a minute before you reward him. Follow the judge's instructions and be aware of what the judge is doing. Don't frustrate the judge by not paying attention to his directions.

The Tibetan Terrier is always judged on the table, so be sure you practice with a grooming table at home before entering the ring.

handlers. Is he moving them up and back, once or twice around, in a triangle?

If possible, you will want to get your number beforehand. Your assigned number must be attached as an armband or with a clip on your outer garment. Do not enter the ring without your number. The ring steward will usually call the exhibits in numerical order. If the exhibits are not called in order, you should strategically place your dog in the line. For instance, if your pup is small for his age, don't stand him next to a large entry; if your dog is reluctant to gait, get at the end of the line-up so that you don't

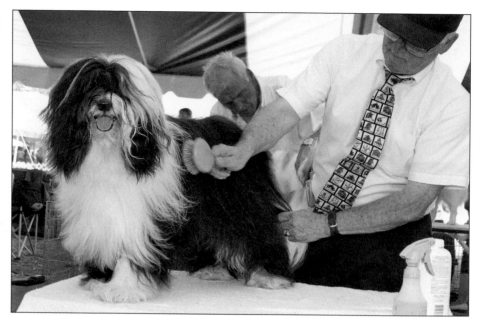

When your dog's turn to be judged arrives, keep him steady and calm. The judge will inspect the dog's bite and dentition, overall musculature and structure and, in a male dog, the testicles, which must completely descend into the scrotum. Likewise, the judge will take note of the dog's alertness and temperament. Aggressiveness is a disqualification in most breeds, and so is shyness. A dog must always be approachable by the judge, even if aloofness is one of the breed's characteristics. Once the judge has completed his hands-on inspection, he will instruct you to gait the dog. A dog's gait indicates to the judge that the dog is correctly constructed. Each breed standard describes the ideal correct gait for that breed. After the judge has inspected all of the dogs in the class in this manner, he will ask the entire class to gait together. He will make his final selections after one last look over the class.

Whether you win or lose, the only one disappointed will be you. Never let your dog know that he's not "the winner." Most important is that you reaffirm your dog's love of the game. Reward him for behaving properly and for being the handsome boy or pretty girl that he or she is.

After your first or second experience in the ring, you will know what things you need to work on. Go home, practice and have fun with your Tibetan

Terrier. With some time and effort, you and your well-trained show dog will soon be standing in the winners' circle with a blue ribbon!

OTHER TYPES OF COMPETITION

In addition to conformation shows, the AKC holds a variety of other competitive events. Obedience trials, agility trials and tracking trials are open to all breeds, while hunting tests, field trials, lure coursing, herding tests and trials, earthdog tests and coonhound events are limited to specific breeds or groups of breeds. The Junior Showmanship program is offered to aspiring young handlers and their dogs, and the Canine Good Citizen® Program is an all-around good-behavior test open to all dogs, pure-bred and mixed.

OBEDIENCE TRIALS

There are three levels of difficulty in obedience competition. The first (and easiest) level is the Novice, in which dogs can earn the Companion Dog (CD) title. The intermediate level is the Open level, in which the Companion Dog Excellent (CDX) title is awarded. The advanced level is the Utility level, in which dogs compete for the Utility Dog (UD) title. Classes at each level are further divided into "A" and "B," with "A" for beginners and "B" for those with more experience. In order to win a title at a given level,

a dog must earn three "legs." A "leg" is accomplished when a dog scores 170 or higher (200 is a perfect score). The scoring system gets a little trickier when you understand that a dog must score more than 50% of the points available for each exercise in order to actually earn the points. Available points for each exercise range between 20 and 40.

A dog must complete different exercises at each level of obedience. The Novice exercises are the easiest, with the Open and finally the Utility levels progressing in difficulty. Examples of Novice exercises are on- and off-lead heeling, a figure-8 pattern, performing a recall (or come), long sit and long down and standing for examination. In the Open level, the Novice-level exercises are required again, but this time without a leash and for longer durations. In addition, the dog must clear a broad jump, retrieve over a jump and drop on recall. In the Utility level, the exercises are quite difficult, including executing basic commands based on hand signals, following a complex heeling pattern, locating articles based on scent discrimination and completing jumps at the handler's direction.

Once he's earned the UD title, a dog can go on to win the prestigious title of Utility Dog Excellent (UDX) by winning "legs" in ten shows. Additionally, Utility Dogs

Not surprisingly,
Tibetan Terriers
perform superbly
in agility trials.

who win "legs" in Open B and Utility B earn points toward the lofty title of Obedience Trial Champion (OTCh.). Established in 1977 by the AKC, this title requires a dog to earn 100 points as well as three first places in a combination of Open B and Utility B classes under three different judges.

Since the days before AKC acceptance, the Tibetan Terrier has excelled at obedience trials, though not in great numbers. The first title winner was Kalyani's Kala Yami of Kyirong, CD, owned by the Corcorans, and she earned the title in June 1965. The first CDX was earned by the very popular "Chubi," formally Luneville Chubitang Kangri, CDX, bred by Angela Mulliner and imported by the Corcorans. In 1977 the UD title was finally added to a Tibetan Terrier: Shergol's Frosted Flake, UD, bred by Bob McCaw and owned by Eileen Conduzio.

AGILITY TRIALS

Agility trials became sanctioned by the AKC in August 1994, when the first licensed agility trials were held. Since that time, agility certainly has grown in popularity by leaps and bounds, literally! The AKC allows all registered breeds (including Miscellaneous Class breeds) to participate, providing the dog is 12 months of age or older. Agility is designed so that the handler demonstrates how well the dog can work at his side. The handler directs his dog through, over, under and around an obstacle course that includes jumps, tires, the dog walk, weave poles, pipe tunnels, collapsed tunnels and more. While working his way through the course, the dog must keep one eye and ear on the handler and the rest of his body on the course. The handler runs along with the dog, giving verbal and hand signals to guide the dog through the course.

The first organization to promote agility trials in the US was the United States Dog Agility Association, Inc. (USDAA). Established in 1986, the US Dog Agility Association, Inc. sparked the formation of many member clubs around the country. To participate in USDAA trials, dogs

must be at least 18 months of age.

The USDAA and AKC both offer titles to winning dogs, although the exercises and requirements of the two organizations differ. Agility Dog (AD), Advanced Agility Dog (AAD) and Master Agility Dog (MAD) are the titles offered by the USDAA, while the AKC offers Novice Agility (NA), Open Agility (OA), Agility Excellent (AX) and Master Agility Excellent (MX). Beyond these four AKC titles, dogs can win additional titles in "jumper" classes: Jumper with Weave Novice (NAJ), Open (OAJ) and Excellent (MXJ). The ultimate title in AKC agility is MACH, Master Agility Champion. Dogs can continue to add number designations to the MACH title, indicating how many times the dog has met the title's requirements (MACH1, MACH2 and so on).

Agility trials are a great way to keep your dog active, and they will keep you running, too! You should join a local agility club to learn more about the sport. These clubs offer sessions in which you can introduce your dog to the various obstacles as well as training classes to prepare him for competition. In no time, your dog will be climbing A-frames, crossing the dog walk and flying over hurdles, all with you right beside him. Your heart will leap every time your dog jumps through the hoop.

TRACKING TIBETANS

The AKC sport of tracking tests a dog's instinctive ability to follow his nose, and licensed trials have been taking place since 1937. The Tibetan Terrier didn't join the ranks of tracking titlists until 1982, when Kyi-rong's Doodle Candy, TD earned the Tracking Dog degree. "Casey," as he was known, was owned and trained by James and Joyce Hill of Missouri. Another breed first was claimed by a top obedience dog named Ch. Kyi-rong's Shanti Kusana, UDT, the first TT to add the tracking degree to a Utility Dog title. She was owned and trained by Ruth Little. Today there are many TTs earning TDs and TDXs, following in the noseprints of these two historical winners.

INDEX

Page numbers in **boldface** indicate illustrations.

My Tibetan Terrier

PUT YOUR PUPPY'S FIRST PICTURE HERE

Dog's Name _____

Date _____ Photographer _____